About Mark Nepo

"Mark Nepo is one of the finest spiritual guides of our time."
—PARKER J. PALMER, author of *The Brink of Everything*
and *The Courage to Teach*

"Mark Nepo is a Great Soul. His resonant heart—his frank and astonishing voice—befriend us mightily on this mysterious trail."
—NAOMI SHIHAB NYE, author of *You and Yours, 19 Varieties of Gazelle: Poems of the Middle East,* and *Red Suitcase*

". . . an eloquent spiritual teacher."
—HERBERT MASON, professor of history and religious thought, Boston University, and translator of *Gilgamesh, A Verse Narrative*

". . . a rare being, a poet who does not overuse language, a wise man without arrogance, a teacher who always speaks with compassion, and an easygoing love-to-listen-to-him storyteller."
—JAMES FADIMAN, PH.D., cofounder, Institute for Transpersonal Psychology

". . . a great storyteller who has much wisdom."
—*Spirituality and Health* magazine

"Mark Nepo's work is as gentle and reliable as the tides, and as courageous as anyone I've known in looking deeply into the mysteries of the self."
—MICHAEL J. MAHONEY, author of *Human Change Processes and Constructive Psychotherapy*

About Mark Nepo's Poetry

"Mark Nepo has a great heart. His poems are good company."
—COLEMAN BARKS, translator of *The Essential Rumi*

"Mark Nepo joins a long tradition of truth-seeking, wild-hearted poets—Rumi, Walt Whitman, Emily Dickinson, Mary Oliver— and deserves a place in the center of the circle with them."
—ELIZABETH LESSER, Cofounder, Omega Institute, author of *Broken Open* and *Marrow*

"These poems touch the soul, reminding each of us what it means to be fully alive, to be surrounded by what is sacred. Allow them to reach under your skin, to where mystery is born into meaning."
—LLEWELLYN VAUGHAN-LEE PH.D., Sufi teacher and author, *Prayer of the Heart*

"Words placed so deliberately yet freely on the page, like Chinese brush strokes on silk . . . Nepo expresses truth . . . in words that inspire and uplift in a sustainable way."
—ANNA JEDRZIEWSKI, *Retailing Insight*

"Brilliant, profound and accessible, [Nepo's] poems are like precious treasures rising from the deep, glistening reminders of what really matters."
—JULIE CLAYTON, *New Consciousness Review*

"Nepo is an inveterate meaning-maker who has delved deeply into the wisdom traditions and the world's religions. In vivid imagery, he captures those connections and epiphanies which illuminate the human condition."
—FREDERIC AND MARY ANN BRUSSAT, *Spirituality and Practice*

The Half-Life of Angels

LIMITED EDITION

ALSO BY MARK NEPO

Nonfiction

Falling Down and Getting Up
Surviving Storms
The Book of Soul
Drinking from the River of Light
More Together than Alone
Things that Join the Sea and the Sky
The One Life We're Given
The Endless Practice
Seven Thousand Ways to Listen
Finding Inner Courage
Unlearning Back to God
The Exquisite Risk
The Book of Awakening

Fiction

As Far As the Heart Can See

Poetry

The Way Under the Way
Inside the Miracle
Reduced to Joy
Surviving Has Made Me Crazy
Suite for the Living
Inhabiting Wonder
Acre of Light
Fire Without Witness
God, the Maker of the Bed, and the Painter

Editor

Deepening the American Dream

Recordings

Falling Down and Getting Up
Surviving Storms
The Book of Soul
Flames that Light the Heart (video course)
More Together Than Alone
The One Life We're Given
Inside the Miracle (expanded, 2015)
Reduced to Joy
The Endless Practice
Seven Thousand Ways to Listen
Staying Awake
Holding Nothing Back
As Far As the Heart Can See
The Book of Awakening
Finding Inner Courage
Finding Our Way in the World
Inside the Miracle (1996)

The
Half-Life
of
Angels

THREE BOOKS OF POEMS

MARK NEPO

FREEFALL BOOKS

Request to cite excerpts from the poems in *The Half-Life of Angels* can be sent to permissions@threeintentions.com.

Cover and interior design by Tabitha Lahr
Cover image by Shutterstock.com
Author photo by Brian Bankston/www.brianbankston.com

FREEFALL BOOKS
Published 2023
Printed in the United States of America

Hardcover: 978-1-7347055-2-2
Ebook: 978-1-7347055-3-9
Library of Congress Control Number: 2023900302

Holy Sites and Ruins

Reading through fifty years of poems has been like stepping through holy sites and ruins in order to map the learnings of all my former selves. This exploration has resurrected old pains and confusions, as well as a sky of mythic images that have come and gone through the center of my heart.

As any poet, I remain dedicated to the retrieval of a deeper, more ancient knowledge that transcends any one self. Yet, such knowledge can only surface through an authentic self. All these expressions have shaped who I am. And traversing this sea of poems, I have met, again, those I have been blessed to love and those who have helped me stay alive.

It's been a challenge to preserve and offer all of this in a way that stays true to the imperfect and messy journey of a soul's unfolding. I kept returning to the structure of my book, *The Way Under The Way*, which contains three books of poems in one volume. I so love that structure that I am relying on it to organize more than 1400 poems into seven such volumes: *The Half-Life of Angels, Unseeable Masters, The Fifth Season, Not Ours To Give, The Heart of No Path, Dropping Pearls Back into the Sea,* and *Easing the Climb.* This is one of those volumes.

I was amazed at how easy it was to see these poems so clearly after so many years. It was obvious when long tales were followed to surface one central insight, and when the excitement of retrieving a metaphor kept me rambling on. Or when two or three poems attached themselves to each other in order to be born. And so, it was swift Tao-like work to separate essence from tangle and to sift what matters from the dirt that was carried along to unearth it. Humbly, for all the craft and skill needed to revise, my advice, after this project, is to simply wait thirty or forty years until your eyes are worn clear.

I have arranged these volumes around periods of work as they came to me through the years. For I have no interest in leaving a trail of polished gems. I can't pretend that I have always perceived as I do now, or that I have always expressed myself as simply or clearly as I do now. So, rather than try to perfect each expression, I have tried to stay true to the developmental voice of each poem, honoring the inner evolution of one spirit in one body in its time on Earth. For the arc of a person inhabiting their full humanness in relation to others and the living Universe is the dynamic poem of a lifetime.

I must also confess that I was moved to see that, in my early work, I would trip into the deep and be completely captivated with a glimpse of what was suddenly in view. Like a marine biologist, I would chronicle the entire dive, culminating with the bit of truth I would find along the bottom. There is nothing wrong with these poems or with this form of inquiry. But it made me realize that now, I live in the deep. And so, my later poems are written through the lens of that depth. I am no longer bringing treasure up to you, but inviting you to risk entering the deep with me. The treasure is in living in the deep. This is the reward of all poetry.

Contents

Book One
A THOUSAND DAWNS

STAYING AFLOAT

Tiger Eye

PATH WORK

THE HOLY DIVIDE

Invisible Mirrors

COATING THE MOON

TO LAND WILDLY

Book Two
THE GODS VISIT

UNDER THE TEMPLE

THE ANCIENT DRIFT

INSIDE THE MUSIC BOX

The One Rain

Close to Finding Our Place

The Bottom
of Heaven

Book Three
The Tone
in the Center
of the Bell

The Loose Dogs
of Santiago

THE METRICS OF SEEING

The Inside of Jade

The Half-Life of Angels

When God is asked in the Torah for His name, a reply comes from the unseeable, "I am Becoming. . . ." At once, "Becoming" emanates two meanings. As a noun, it suggests that God is a process, that the sacred reveals itself in a life of transformation and unfolding that never ends. As a verb, it suggests that God is still emerging, still not completely defined, beautifully as unfinished as we are.

By saying His name is "I am Becoming," God is showing us how to live fully in the world. This suggests that the aim of any sacred becoming is not to arrive at any finished state, but to taste everything in our brush with life and thereby know, through experience, the spark of what is holy.

The kind of courage this requires is both real and noble. Real in the fact that the only way to "become" is through facing our experience directly and to commit to our continual emergence. And noble in how we stay faithful to what is possible if we keep sparking tomorrow with who we are today. The Persian poet of the thirteenth century, 'Aṭṭār, affirms this kind of courage when he says, "For your Soul, seek Spiritual knowledge from what is Real."

This spark of becoming is the synapse between living things. This spark of becoming is the half-life of angels that arcs between the deer's nose and the thawed stream, between Sappho's heart and the poems she uttered, between God's finger and Adam's hand, and between the Ocean of Source and the lips of every soul. In time, the soul's journey in the world strips away all that is extraneous—the way a meteor is stripped to its essence of light as it catapults toward Earth. It can take a lifetime to burn off what doesn't matter until we face each other—spark to spark.

The three books of poems in this collection explore and praise this life-giving spark.

Book One

A THOUSAND DAWNS

To harden will help us get through life,
but to soften will let us experience life.

—MN

The Heart Is
Still Our Teacher

The old world is gone and still,
one candle can light many, if we
work with what we're given and
resist the suffering in not suffering.

The daily work is to remember
that you can't fly with one wing.

During adversity, we finally accept
that our kinship is to meet below
all names.

No matter how we stray, we are
taught by the rush of life that,
in the thick of it, we are always
moving toward a greater sense
of living.

It is the blessing of the ordinary
that awakens us to everything.

Staying Afloat

Every day a somewhat different interfusion.
Today I feel sadness along with appreciation.
I feel disappointment along with delight.
I sense light penetrating heaviness.
Will I allow these ways to swirl together
Into another blend that can wash through my soul?

—GAIL WARNER

Like It or Not

Suffering is the bow that plays
the heart. It makes me ache in
a place I knew before birth, a
place we share but only access
when alone.

If we accept the rub, we can hold
each other up to all that life offers.
Perhaps this is the purpose of
suffering, to let music rise.

In time, our suffering sinks like
a stone plopped in a lake,
changing everything, though
it is never seen again.

Close

Often, what matters doesn't
reach us until the crisis is over.

How close we were to life or
death makes us tremble weeks
later while watching a goldfinch
eat from the feeder.

Then, we wonder what we're
doing and if it's worth all
we've put on hold.

Is anything worth this moment
asking to be entered, the way
a waterfall is asked to find
its ledge?

Depth Finder

While we marvel at the dolphin
or whale breaking surface, this great
leap is followed by a great surrender
back into what no one can see.

These surges of power are always
followed by a letting go.

Like the whale, we are never done.
Like the dolphin, we nose our way
into the world, only to plummet
back into the deep.

The Art of Netting

This is how it works. I almost die.
You're at my side. It's hard on you.
And so, your friend is at your side.

Next month or year, it's you who
falls into the crater. Then, I'm there
for you. And my old friend is there
for me.

This is how a net distributes the
weight. How the net of hearts
distributes the suffering.

Even our dog climbing my wife's
lap when she cries is part of the net.

We Try So Hard

We cling to everything—clothes,
memories, dreams—so tightly when
only burning them will warm us.

We want so badly to come alive
when to do so we must die along
the way.

And finding love, we want to hide
it like a treasure at the bottom of
the sea. Instead life humbles us
to be the flag to each other's wind.

Never Gone

The truth that outlasts us rises
like sun through morning trees.
It's always there. Like the thing
that unravels once pain stops.
Never gone. Only diverted. Like
water over branches. Like love
meandering through trouble.
So, though you're face down,
look up. Even when our eyes
are closed, the sun still warms.

Held in Place

I'm sipping coffee in a mug my wife
threw on her wheel, while our dog
sleeps near me. The morning rain
is clearing and I think of friends,
near and far, here and gone, as the
coffee warms my throat. The slightest
sway of life between us is astonishing,
as the weight of the planet held
in place by a burning star. As the
weight of a life such as mine, held
in place by this burning love
that tethers me to others.

The Difference

When knotted, we feel the tug,
the pull, and all our attention
goes to where we are tied.

To free ourselves, we have to
go to the spaces in the knot
and breathe.

Often, the difference between
Heaven and Hell is how a turtle
slips beneath its weight
into the water.

In Her Way

In the parking lot, she
helped an old man with
his groceries. And near
the drugstore, she helped
a little girl find her dog.
The next day, she put
a starfish back into
the sea. And yesterday,
she gave old clothes to
strangers. Once home,
an old friend who was
drowning called and she
listened him ashore. All
the while, she ached to
be of use. Like the sun,
unaware of its light, she
longs to help small
things grow.

Call of
the Voiceless

Worlds collapse. Mountains
avalanche. The sea can rise to
decimate a village. And men can
lose their minds, killing everything
in sight, in a last attempt to feel.

Yet, it is the gentle push that no
one sees that enables us to reach
the other side where despair begins
to dissipate like a fog that
can no longer block the path.

Rope and Slats

Between doubt and clarity
there is a bridge made of rope
and slats that we must cross
repeatedly, for it's the view
that lets things clear.

We mustn't argue on that
bridge or we will fall.

Besides, the view is not
debatable, only seeable.

The Work
of Care

I'm not sure I can help
but my heart wants to try.

Oh, I can shop for you or
bring you dinner.

I can even help you up
should you fall.

But when the hunger is
inside, when the break is
where no one can see,

then all we can do is
be a greenhouse for
each other.

Take These Teachers

To outlast our pain is to endure,
the way an orchid opens after a storm.

To love without thought of reward
is like a tiger erupting in its leap.

To accept that there's nowhere to go
is like an elephant balancing on the
tip of a diamond.

Take these teachers into your heart
and they will open the cage of your
mind, letting the dove of your worth
flutter.

Beyond All Reach

We can try to avoid being touched
by life and never live. Or reach into
the storm and lose an arm, only to
have something deeper grow from
its stub.

A new tree grows from its stump.
A new love grows from the break
in our heart. No one likes this.
No one seeks this.

It is how life pries us open, so
the gem hidden in our mountain
can surface after the avalanche.

Oh, there is sweetness, too. But
sweetness needs no preparation
other than a willingness to be
softened by the flower that
opens in our throat, forcing
us to whisper "Ah."

Back and Forth

The caterpillar has to bunch
to move forward.

The bird has to drop its wings
in order to pump higher.

And the dolphin has to dive
in order to breach.

Is it any wonder that we
need to know sorrow
in order to know joy?

For Paul

There is no understanding
why you and Linda had to
suffer, only to lose her.

Now, you meet her in the things
you loved, with no way back and
no way forward, just this hole
in your heart through which
life keeps blowing.

Strangely, you are not being
asked to stitch the loss closed,
for that is impossible.

Now, there is only the vast
emptiness, a tribute to the size
of the love you shared, which
stops us, the way we dizzy at the
edge of the Grand Canyon.

Like That

I can't take away
your pain or save you
from your life.

But holding the one
who is suffering is the
only raft we have.

Putting your palm on
the surface of a lake, you
can feel the entire lake.
Compassion is like that.

By the River

A weary soul kneels by the river,
plunging his hands in despair.
Miles away, another kneels to
wash her sorrows.

Without ever knowing, they give
to each other, the way electricity
illumines two bulbs that think
they are the only light.

Love works this way: a river that
helps each other rise, a charge
that makes each other glow.

The web of kinship is as vast as
the cries of constellations across
the dark.

And the dreams we choose from
shimmer like stars in an inward
sky. They wait for the frightened
thing in us to wake, that we might
bring them into the world.

Once Stopping

After two tours in Iraq,
he can't close his eyes without
hearing shells blast in his skin.

After growing up with all that
anger, she can't sit under the moon
without hearing them rage.

It's true, silence has to swallow all
that has happened before it can
baptize us.

Then, like flamingoes who
land in Mumbai after migrating
for days from the Sambhar
Lake in Rajasthan,

we tuck our long beaks into
our chests and feel the sky
carry us, even on the ground.

Feeding the Fire

Skip has written his first blues
song. And George has added
more vegetables to his garden.

And Don keeps following his
endless watercolors.

While Paul stitches hearts torn
by the journey.

And David outlasts his father's
complaints while healing
children in Africa.

While Tom builds owl boxes
on the land he loves.

When awake, we feed
the soul its kindling.

Marathon

Like a runner
unable to catch
his breath, we're
not sure where
the race is going.

We stop for love
like water at the
twenty-mile marker
and some of us
never go on.

And once in a
while, when some
wild-eyed youngin'
asks, we sigh and
think,

We all tumble
till we cascade,
afraid of living,
afraid of dying,
afraid of rising,
afraid of falling.

But we say only
that life is beautiful
and hard.

On the Precipice

Just when it's too hard to find
a way, when I can't turn off the
pain, something lifts in the world
or from my eyes. And I am, again,
among those eager to live. How
does this happen? I stop trying
to understand and let myself be
shaken from my darkness. For,
in this moment, I am like a small
gem carried in the mouth of an
angel. I pray it will cleanse me
and drop me back into my life.

Aprilis

I never tire of Spring, the spray
of color inching from the ground,
the eddies of wind lifting our faces.

Every dog in the neighborhood knows
something is coming alive. They jump
at nothing and roll in the grass. As
robins and finch and bluebirds
keep twigging their nests.

Suddenly, we begin to dream again,
of small things and large, of repairing
the bench crippled in winter or of
starting a new life, by leaving
or staying. It doesn't matter.

The Earth is opening again.
Saying we can, too.

To and From

When falling down,
the hurt seems big
and I feel small.

But Life waits
to fill everything,
like light entering
the pinhole of a shell.

And Truth enters my
mind the way light
floods that pinhole.

I am reborn
the instant I accept
that what's in my hand
has been everywhere.

Taking Wing

Each day is a chance to
be here more completely.
Each day, like waking after
a long journey.

On the inside, every day is
a lifetime. Each morn we are
born. Each night we die.

And nothing matters but
opening the wings of our
heart as far as we can.

At the end of each burden,
the sudden awareness that life
is closer than we thought.

To Seek

They call it nose work when dogs
find things by the power of their
scent. And the great white shark,
older than the dinosaur, can smell
a single drop of blood floating in
ten billion drops of water.

And the silk moth can track a single
pheromone in another moth seven
miles away. While a grizzly can find
a pocket of honey a hundred
times faster than a human.

But the African elephant has the
strongest sense of smell. It will trek
a thousand miles to nuzzle a lost
or dead member of its herd.

So, despite our plans, it is the heart
that works like a bloodhound: sniffing
out what is hidden, seeking a drop
of truth in the ocean of days.

To Go Beyond

You ask, "How can I hold on?"
I remember being forced to let
go, to let the torrent take me
beyond all I could imagine.

You ask, "Are we doomed to
repeat our mistakes?" I only know
that when exhausted I could finally
accept that we are privileged to
have more than one chance
to come alive.

You ask, "Why is it all unbearable?"
I want to rock you until you under-
stand that the dark is there
for light to find its purpose.

You ask if I have anything to say.
And I touch my forehead to yours,
hoping something in all that is un-
sayable will skip like a stone along
the waters of the One Mind.

Erosion

On a still morning, you
may stumble and wonder
why you're carrying
what you're carrying,
why you're never
where you are.

It seems a trick: to feel
so much and not be able
to hold it. But the clouds
can't hold the sun and
the waves can't hold
the wind.

When worn of our secrets,
we become temporary
blessings, like flags worn
free of their signs.

Lose your grip on what you
want and what others tell you
you want, and life becomes
simple. There is less to do.
Like a pearl washed ashore,
we just wait to be found.

Staying Afloat

Each of us is a raft at sea.
When solo, it's all we can
do to keep from being
thrown under.

But like the floating villages
in the East China Sea, we
can tie our rafts together
in order to survive.

So, if you spot me bobbing,
tie your raft to mine. We
can build a home in the
vastness and drift.

I Need to Know

How the willow catches the wind
without falling over, so I can leave
the house.

How birds sing at the first sign of
light, so I can stop living in the past.

How starfish grow another point,
so wounds won't cripple me.

How elephants find their way to
the river, so nothing will stop me
from living my life.

TIGER EYE

I will bear my loneliness
like a planet that cannot
deny its orbit around
the pull of what is true.

—MN

The Hamster Wheel

Under all this stress, the wheel
cracks and, breathing hard, I
stare at the world beneath my task.

Now, I look for the world beneath
everything and wonder, why all this
running?

When pressed, I feel like a fugitive.
When seeing through, I am
an explorer.

In My Study

The light from the sun
moves through the red maple,
through my window, and onto
my desk, where the shadow of
the leaves sways over this page.

I think to trace the leaves but
that won't capture the light.
So, I simply watch, grateful
for this scratch of the ineffable.

Red Hawk Glide

Almost awake, my heart lifts like
a red hawk gliding over the open field
we call the past. And there, the fence
I built, all broken by that storm no
one saw coming. And by the river,
the scenes of those bringing me back
to life. And the campfires which held
so many stories, peppered across time.
The smoke of their lessons forms the
clouds I glide through. I can barely
make out the faces of those I loved.
Having circled what some call a life,
the red hawk lands back in my chest,
somewhere between what has been
and what will be. And I wake amid
leaves that rustle, to so many things
to do.

Losing Someone

After the rip of having your heart
pulled from your chest,
                        grief turns us
into an icicle in March, one unending
tear thinning everything until we fall
attached to nothing.

To Suffer Time

From the inside, everything
makes sense, which is why
we were born with a heart
and two ears.

It is staying on the outside
that breeds fear and
violence.

The greatest courage, then,
is to put everything down
and wait.

Like a flag for its wind.

To Uncover

If we can outlast feeling
indignant when knocked
to our knees, it will become
clear that we've never been
this close to the earth.

And when our walls come
down, we can be humbled
by the truth that they were
unnecessary.

For all the ways we hammer
and prop things up, it is
listening that allows
us to change.

I braid the silence between
us to affirm that we are
of the same tribe.

You Have Trouble with My Story

Every day, we stand on the verge of trimming every-
thing to fit our mind or joining with the presence
of everything that is not us. History is the record of
cutting everything down or letting everything in. So,
when I share something older than time, don't dismiss
it as my story. Come closer and stay in conversation
with the part of the story that taps on your heart.
When I share the wonder, don't say you can't find it
on your map. Stay longer and let the doe grazing on
the edge of the forest lead you. When I marvel at what
can't be named, don't exile it with your pragmatism.
Ask more questions. A waterfall can't be captured in
a bucket, any more than the Living Universe can be
ordered into a worldview.

No Vacancy

If you can't dip your cup
into the stream, how can
you fill it with water?

If you can't bend your
emptiness toward life, how
can you drink of the days?

If you keep your thoughts
caged like bees, you will
only know their buzz.

If you never let your thoughts
find their way, how can they
bring you honey?

You can't ride truth like a
horse, nor can you saddle
your life.

The Party
of Your Life

Always invite Death to your table
but never let him choose the meal.

Give him plenty of wine.
He only pretends to keep secrets.

Be sure to listen past the drama.
He will try to make it all about you.

But once it gets late and he stops
spinning tales, once everyone leaves,

he will grow quiet as a lake under the
stars. Look him in the eye then and
he will mirror the Mysteries of Life.

Be kind to him for he is lonely, too,
but never let him stay over. Keep
him warm but call him a cab.

The Work of Being

Everyone wants me to tame this
deeper presence into a purpose,
but below all that, what matters
won't obey my command. It's
more like the swell of the
ocean.

It lifts me and drops me as
the sun fills my face, with
no place to go, only
this call to live.

Tiger Eye

I've been told my whole life
that survival is all that matters,
that we better hunker down.

But watching animals leap
and run, they seem so holy
and uncomplicated.

And just yesterday, the eagle's
chest grew whiter so as not to
be seen by its prey, while the
white pine held its excess
water like a jewel in the sun.

I realize now that each of us
is born with a light that can't
go out and an unquenchable
need to stand up and go on.

Just look at the constancy
of a hummingbird before
a flower twice its size.

I can see, at last, that far
enough in: shining forth
and surviving are the same.

In India, legend has it that
the soul of the world makes
a tiger's stripes fade over
time. As kindness wears
away our distrust.

Yet Again

I told your story again
to someone who didn't
know you.

Of how you were sent
to London from Lithuania
ahead of the war.

Of how I met you when
you were eighty.

Of how you took my hand
and said, "Tell me what
you care about."

I pass you on like a star
or firefly that can only
be seen in the dark.

Impromptu

We're taught that misfortune
is back luck, but the pilgrim who
stumbles in this life clears the way
for the one who wakes in the next.

And every time my heart breaks,
I rediscover that kinship outweighs
all manner of thinking.

So dance with me, though we're
both winded and lame. For nothing
is as daring as opening our life
to what moves through us.

Given all the time there is or no
time at all, I will live the same,
carrying only what my armless
heart can bear.

Inside the Lotus

Centuries ago, some carver
chiseled the markings on this
Ganesh who sits with his near
hand raised, palm up.

I put my palm to the wooden
palm and touch what he touched,
a thousand years later.

Somehow, all the suffering in
those years arcs to me. And the
wooden palm seems to say, "Now
that you know, stop. Now that you
feel everything, put it down."

The lesson of the ages: not
to carry but to let through.

Ancient Lesson

I have been humbled and
made bare by great love
and great suffering.

I have since learned how
to still the storm by dropping
the ten thousand things.

What little peace I have
comes from not picking
them up.

PATH WORK

Love and suffering carry us
from our small path
to the big path
where all life meets.

—MN

The Life
After Tears

In the life before tears,
there are endless plans
and we avoid the difficult
feelings at all cost, as if grief,
pain, and loss are canyons
we'll never climb out of.

But, then, one day, while
not looking, someone dear
dies, or a dream breaks like
a plate, and our world, as
we've known it, is blown
apart.

Then, we discover that
falling in the canyon is
our initiation, and
the river at the bottom
is the only water that
will keep us alive.

I wish it were different.
But the reward for being
hollowed out is that the
song then sings us.

The Unseen Path

Looking back, there is a
trail that was not visible
going forward.

Looking back, I can see
that like sudden light that
parts the cloud, my honesty,
when found, has cleared
my confusion.

Like all song that ends in
silence, the truth, when
found, has brought us
together.

Like wood that keeps
the fire going, my care
has lit the way.

Hidden Symmetries

Her mother died. His father is adrift.
My godchild's daughter is learning how
to draw. And a friend of a friend calls
unable to find his way. And another,
who had gone down a more solitary
path, sends a prayer shawl from Tibet.
I then learn quite by chance that my
college roommate has lost his daughter.
And the gentle one who protested the
last war drops his head as his son enlists.
With every step, we create more chances.
Now, the quiet one in Canada is learning
Sanskrit, while the one who lost his job
is building a barn. Some call what can't
be planned a nest of dangers. I call it the
kaleidoscope of life which stains us with
each other's deepest colors. And I would
have your yellow if you will drink my blue.

Pathfinder

Were I a guide, I'd walk
to the end of all maps and
smile. If a dancer, I'd long
to dance the ground before
the pyramids were built. If a
sculptor, I'd watch the wind
sculpt the face of the sea. If
a troubled monk, I'd plant
silence like seeds and wait.
If a tired soldier, I'd steal
the guns at night and bury
them in water, so there'd
be nothing to dig for
when we wake.

To Stand
and Serve

They also serve who
only stand and wait.

—JOHN MILTON

The small island in the middle
of the ocean only shows itself
when the waters recede, the
way a sage is only wise when
the noise subsides.

And the path in the forest
remains hidden until the sun
spills through the trees, the
way the path of love seems
out of reach until we let the
undying light escape from
our hearts.

Gone Fishin'

Bears swipe at salmon
in the river and wood–
peckers drill their heads
silly for what's under the
bark.

As lonely souls swipe
and drill the days for love.

Somehow all life knows
that what sustains
lives below.

But who was the first to
throw a line overboard
and hope to bring up
something from the deep?

What did they see or feel
that made them row out
from shore and wait?

The Art
of Saxifrage

When exhausted of my pain,
I chance into wonder and stand
between the endless signs of life
and the endless ash of dreams.

In those moments, I realize that
to make it through the cascade
of rip and repair that we call life
is astonishing, like a wildflower
surviving winter on a canyon wall.

Yet we do. And once we learn the
art of saxifrage, it's clear. The only
thing that wears down stone with
its constant trickle is kindness.

I'm coming to see that to prevent
stealing, we need to give until
there's nothing left to take.

Markers

Like a hiker who leaves small markers along the trail
for others, so they won't miss the narrow path to the
left that leads to the hidden waterfall—each of us is
surrounded by markers of this life. Around me now:
my father's awl, which I hold to feel what he held,
great maker that he was. And there, a jar of sand
from Coney Island, given to me by Chari because
our grandmothers came from the same village out-
side of Kiev. And this hand-carved stamp I bought
in Chinatown in San Francisco, which cracked on
the way home, so cleanly I have never glued it. It
rests perfectly in place to remind me how imperfect
we are. And balanced on my bookcase, the sculpted
piece of driftwood that washed to my feet on the
shore of St. Martin weeks after cancer washed me
ashore. Next to it, a small stone from the Red Sea
given to me in Amsterdam by a woman drowning in
her cancer. And on the small table to my right, my
grandfather's prayer book, brought with him from
Russia, which I hold to feel the vastness that defies
all words. When I simply follow the markers and
breathe, I remember that Heaven is wherever we
stop and open time.

Three Paths

I had fallen. When I got up, there
were three paths I hadn't seen.

One went down to the river where
the rhythm of life eased the current.

The far path went into the mountains,
away from the living, where the birds
of prey were tired of looking for prey.

The middle path led back into the
world, where I belonged, though
I wanted to take the other two.

A Pause in Our Song

Someone in deep grief rings a bell
in a field where no one can hear.
It makes the birds pause in their
song and the willows slouch a little
closer to the ground. She just keeps
ringing it until the ancient tone
draws her back into the world.

At the same time, someone who
has lost his purpose sits on a bench
underground, watching those like
him board and leave the subway.
He searches for his resolve as if he's
lost his wallet. Despite his alarm, he
has a creeping sense that sitting on
this bench underground is a spot
of Heaven.

I understand them both. For I have
let the crack in my heart ring where
no one can hear. And I have found
peace in the center of being lost.

Path Work

What light is for plants,
love is for souls.

It is that which causes
us to grow and that
toward which we grow.

As a seed inches under-
ground toward a light
it can't yet see,

love and suffering
cause us to break
ground and flower.

We break ground by
following our heart,
by being real, and
being kind.

This stirring to
break ground
and flower is
our transformation.

I welcome it by any
name. It has saved
my life.

The Flight of Consciousness

At first, the bird, no matter its
size, is startled to fly. At once, the
dizziness of up and down. Then, the
awe and wonder of glide and sheer
intoxication of the sky. Until in the
throes of migration, there is the long
weight of being alone. Beyond this,
the descent back to the nest,
where everything is the same,
but different.

Soft Histories

When the forsythias shout yellow
and the shadblow utter their white,
I brew some coffee and move the
chair to the patch of deck that
stays warm all morning.

There I sit like a small statue about
to come alive. Until everything slows.
The birds seem to hover, the flowers
swallow their dew, and a deeper wind
stirs the dead. Their dreams reach us
first, then their soft histories,
so much like our own.

And when the living and the dead
come together like two hands clapping,
a song of Heaven opens, common
as a hidden path agreeing to
show itself to the world.

Ageless

Like a cliff we climb
to take in the sea,

art and music mark
the path we climb

to see how all lives
are connected.

And poetry is
the small pool
we drink from

that fills us with
the truth that we
are the same.

Doing and Undoing

We hack a path through what we
don't know, so we might get closer
to the unmarked nature of things.
But our wandering becomes a trail
which, in time, we need to wander
from. It's the same with ideas.

In time, our well-worn thoughts
keep us from the wildness of
what matters.

All this is necessary: wandering
till we clear a path, then feeling
confined by the path, till we
break our own rules.

The aim of a path is to find its
end, so we can start a new path.

What Comes from Being Joined

My old friend, Tom, took my wife, Susan, and I to the natural cathedral of redwoods in Henry Cowell State Park near Santa Cruz, California. I so wanted Susan to be there. The look on her face before these ancient, silent elders was worth the trip cross-country. The light sprayed through the canopy on the fan-like ferns, as if to say, "The secret of all paths is that they undo themselves to Here."

Across the way, a small fawn stepped between two redwoods and the unblocked light bathed it in a moment that opened all time. I whispered to Tom, "That's what we're all after."

No matter what we dream or scheme or where we strive to land, it is all for the moment when the light opens us briefly to Eternity. No one can plan this. We can only inhabit it when it appears.

A little further in, we came upon two gnarly redwoods that had grown side by side for the first fifty years. Then, about a hundred feet up, they had merged as one tree for another fifty years. Then, another hundred feet up, they began to grow separately again. They seemed a great teacher of how intimacy shapes us. How we are drawn to the depth and center of another and, in time, this leads us to join as one. If we stay true enough and live long enough, the fiber of our oneness allows us to grow separately again, on the other side of intimacy. We grow together, if given time, only to grow apart while rooted in our togetherness.

I looked at Susan whom I have lived with for twenty-seven years, and at Tom whom I have been friends with for twenty-five years—and I knew this mystery of growth to be true. The individuation that leads us to each other is different than the humility and authority of being that come from being joined. Yet both are holy. The light filtered on the faces of my loved ones. And I wondered if we looked as holy to the fawn as she did to us.

Outstretch
Your Arms

Along the way, people we love
fall from the tightrope and vanish
and we wonder, why not me?

Then, there is a pandemic and
thousands cough and die with
no warning.

Or simply getting older, the view
widens but the path narrows. As
if we're dancing on the edge of
a cliff.

But it has always been this way.
We are only now aware of it.

This is what the ancients were
honoring when they painted
their faces and danced around
the fire.

As if pain is the bark and joy
is the sap.

What other dance is there?

Worth the Work

My hips burn as I climb the path,
using roots as steps, but the view
is worth the work, always.

The way we climb questions until
we're out in the open, able to
take in what we seldom see.

This is the purpose of questions,
to help us climb into the open.
Though, often, the heart burns
as we open.

This is not the pain of injury
but the pain of exercise. Like
pressing weights, we lift what-
ever's in the way.

Only to put it down behind
us, not to deprive the next
seeker their climb, their work,
their training.

The Holy Divide

The world [is] not to be put in order: the world is order incarnate.
It is for us to put ourselves in unison with this order.

—Henry Miller

The transcendence of duality is the inheritance of all mystics . . .
the fullest wisdom is to see everything as sacred.

—Rachel Jamison Webster

Destined

We are. But in the way that
flowers are destined to open,
or that waves are destined to
fold on themselves and gather.

Fate is not the arrow of our secret
ambition, but the turning of a life
around an unshakable center, the
way the Earth turns on its axis in
its journey around the sun.

So, when I confess that we are meant
for each other, I am not singling us out
from the thousands of lovers who have
stumbled through the centuries.

But more, that you are the rain that
opens my petal. And in that moment
of unfolding, we are touched in the
one spot that everyone who ever
loved has known.

Inside the Fable

How is it that when alone,
I want to be with you? And
when with you, I want to
be alone?

And when here, I want to
be there. And once there,
I want to be here.

Why does it take a close call
to give up all calls? And a great
storm to make me stop?

Why an immense calm to make
me open where I seldom open?

When I truly see you, I begin
to accept myself.

And when you reach for me,
despite my failings, I wait like
a tree for you to land and
build us a nest.

Notes While Meditating

As I close my eyes, I can see the young man pouring my coffee at Starbucks, the steam circling his hands; myself doing the dishes at home, the water running; my wife talking to the scheduler at the doctor's office, her soft hands jotting down the time; can see our dog sleeping belly up. With each breath, I'm moving back and forth from moments in the world to the glow of my breathing. I'm aware of the crow outside though it has stopped cawing. I miss my grandmother. Suddenly I can see Gaudi's unfinished cathedra in Barcelona, more beautiful because the inside of worship faces the world. I walk around unfinished, my insides facing the world. I begin to find comfort in slightly rocking. While rocking, I don't have to choose between inner and outer. Like the ancient rabbis I had no idea I was connected to, like the old Jews I watched sway on Saturday mornings, I discover that rocking while opening my heart lets the God within meet the God without. Some days, my soul feels like an inlet with a large stone stuck in its throat.

Nada y Todo

(Spanish for nothing and everything)

This phrase was etched by hand
in wood over the door to the Hermitage
where everyone lives in silence.

I went there to clear my mind.
In dropping into the vastness, I could
see that each of us lives in the holy
clearing between nothing and
everything.

Once there, I could see that only
when viewing nothing from everything
do we fear it. And only when viewing
everything from nothing do we feel
impoverished.

But no life is small on the inside.

Sojourner

If we think what matters
is yet to come, we will
sell all we have to buy
a ticket to the future.

If thinking God is
in the darkness, we will
burn the truth to light
our way.

And believing in less,
we'll be convinced that
the light is in you instead
of me, and tear each other
apart in search of our
worth.

None of this is helpful.
To never admit that the
miracle is where we are
has brought down empires.

Better to listen to the deep
in all directions and
live by the sea.

The Work of Love

If I could, I'd reach into your heart,
as I would a hole in the earth, and
pull out the dark thing that eats at
you. If I could, I'd drag it out of
you and leave it in the sun where
it would stop showing its teeth
and go to sleep.

Then, I hope you would do the
same for me.

Mitosis

When breathing
through our fear, we
grow toward each other.

And when a whale
breaches a wave for light,
it is revealed, for one long
moment, how love can
make us better than we
are.

The way a cell divides
and grows, true question
halves the mind until the
heart flowers through
all thought.

Until, against our will,
we open like flowers
after a storm.

For Linda

A friend has died, ripped from us
with the harshness of a tornado no
one saw coming. I am aimless, restless,
unsure what to do. As I wander through
the house, many are dying and many are
being born. Each a stitch in the ribbon
of time. Some will pass each other on
the street. Some will fall in love and
give birth to others. Some will know
ease while others will be burdened.
Then, we'll take turns. Each will try
to write their name in the sky. A few
will accept that we come and go, while
most will ask why. I wander in the yard,
looking for a sign of what might last,
only to find Linda's grace in a puddle,
in the sky reflected in the puddle, and
in the grief reflected in my heart. Now,
another storm, another clearing,
another day of sun. Who can
keep up?

The Native Self

We tumble into existence,
trying to sustain the wonder
of first arriving, trying to ride
the angel when in time we have
to accept that the angel rides us.

Each of us is gifted and desperate
and the great battle is to dive
through our desperation
into our gift.

This is the journey of the native
self: to pass by the dragon and,
most of all, to stop being
the dragon.

No matter how we twist or
dream, the indifference of
all this beauty says, "You
are not little gods, but many
chambered gates. If you stay
open, I will flood you
with all you need."

Riddle of Will

When I finally looked inside,
I was my own witness.

—Skip Lee

We are born to witness but taught
to watch. And the watcher judges
while the witness accepts.

In time, we wander like two monks
cursing the journey, until they fall
in the mud. Once in the mud, they
start laughing at their endless rise
and fall.

To accept the journey is to be
a smooth pebble. To love the
journey is to bend like a fish in
a current that goes everywhere
and nowhere.

Within

Within the mountain
the stream runs clear;
out of the mountain
it turns to mud.

—Tu Fu

Within our heart, the love is
clear. In the world, it gathers
everything it touches. Like
honey spilled in dirt.

In the antechamber we call
the mind, concepts remain
possible, until we voice them.

Then, like fish glimpsed
in the shallows, we try to
grab them.

The world is not fallen, only
heterogeneous. Like a carnival
whose tents are always flapping,
whose rides are always open.

Undermost

Afraid of dying, we run.
Afraid of living, we hide.

The pull of running and
hiding ties us in knots.

All the while, our soul waits
for us to tire of the chase.

All the while, the center of
trouble waits like a cloud
to be dispersed by a light
that has no name.

The Holy Divide

When too close to others,
I lose the path to silence,
forgetting how to sit
with what matters.

When still enough, I can
hear the sigh of the very
planet as it grunts its
way through the dark.

Then, I can't imagine
climbing back into the
world.

We all cross this holy divide,
the way we sleep and wake,
the way we move from day
to night,

the way we feel certain of
things that can't be said
and at a loss how to bring
their medicine to all the
break and ruin around us.

Wait Long Enough

Ch'u Yuan, the early song poet
of China, wrote *The Question
of Heaven* after seeing murals
scrawled on temple walls.
They wouldn't let him be.

2400 years later, I scrawl this,
still pondering his question:
"What closes in to bring
evening? What opens out
to bring morning?"

And who will pick up this
pebble stuck in my heart?
Ch'u drowned himself in
the Mi-Lo River at the age
of sixty-two. Was he
opening or closing?

Each of us who dares to look,
who dares to ask, becomes a
ripple. Wait long enough
and each soul is a one-
stringed harp keeping
the same note going.

The Ancestors
Tell Us Where
They've Gone

Can an entire life escape
through a rip or pop in its body?

We desperately try but can't
put the song back into the bird.

We look for them everywhere
and follow their sweetness

like the ghosted tracks of a deer
that has become the forest.

A Lost Myth

There was a man afraid to live.
To cure his fear, he was turned
into a bird imprisoned in a cloud.
And only when he opened his
heart would the cloud part.

Only then would he turn back
into a person. Years went by
and he drifted like a secret
in the center of a storm.

Every spring, his sorrow
would build until the cloud
he lived in would darken
and shower the earth.

Finally, he exhausted his
fear and fell from the sky
where he became a fire
with no home.

And from his ash, the
person waiting inside
all those years
began to form.

All the Same

We forget that in the
beginning, the seed,
the soil, and tip of
root are one.

And so, when reduced
to our beginnings, love
and truth interlace.

When cleaved of our
opinions, you and I are
one seed, waiting for
the sun to unfurl us.

Pendulum

(a weight hung
from a fixed point)

For my first house,
my father made a wooden
clock with a pendulum.

When I left that marriage,
I packed the clock carefully,
wrapping the pendulum
separately, and hung the
clock in my apartment,
near the bay window.

But the echo of its tick
kept time with my failures.

So, I stopped it in the night
and loved time more, once
it was quiet.

When my oldest friend
retired after thirty years,
I bought an old watch
from Good Will and
smashed its face.

I sent it to him as my wish
for both of us to leap into
all that is timeless.

Now, I long to stop the
clock I carry inside, to
stop the pendulum that
swings from my neck,
that keeps measuring
life instead of living it.

Dusting Off

In ancient China, it was
an avalanche that blocked
the pass for months.

During the terrible war,
it was the occupation that
kept families apart for years.

In our age, it is a disease
that moves quicker than
all hesitation.

And coming up from the
rubble, the light draws us
out.

As we pray to the same
gods who turned their backs,
asking that they blow our
catastrophes aside, letting
us stir again.

When You Can

We cry when we long for love
and cry when we lose it. This
is how we open and close
the wings of the heart.

Only when the hand grips
nothing does it become a fist.

So, when you can, put something
in your hand: a tool or another's
dream.

After you rebuild what has fallen
or broken or been taken away,
put what you can't carry
on the path for others.

What to Do?

Life can turn in a second.
Yes, the car can crash but
the sun can also come through
just in time to meet the one
you'll spend your life with.

So, we can stay inside
and try to avoid the crash
but then we'll never meet
the one who will hold our
head through the storm.

What to do?

It is said the old condor,
unable to speak its wisdom,
closes its eyes when it glides
above the Andes.

Those in trouble
take this as a sign.

Unraveled

It's as if God squeezes this
beautiful, terrible day like a
lemon and those caught in
the grip grow so tender that
there is nowhere left to go.

Others, not caught in the
squeeze, don't understand.
There are things to do and
bills to pay.

But all the plans against disaster
have been squeezed out of you
and the bee nuzzling its face
in the nectar of the peony
seems now like the end
of all our questions.

Into the Gap

From the Egyptian slave who helped
his other up from the mud, to those
in the revolution bringing a chunk of
bread to the fallen, to you holding me
all those years ago when I was throwing
up from chemo, to the out-of-work chef
bringing the old painter meals on Sunday.
Such giving is the unbreakable synapse
that keeps the Universe going. After
falling down enough, we realize: this
is our destiny, to charge with care
across the gap between living things.

The Clearing

I had climbed beyond what
I knew, in search of something
lasting, and far away from the
crowd, I found this clearing
from which I glimpsed life
outside of my own story.

And life was never more
revealing, though I couldn't
stay there, any more than a
bird can nest in the sun.

So, I came back into the
world, though I'm never far
from that clearing. I carry it
within like a candle lit from
the great unending fire.

And when exhausted of my
thoughts, I find the clearing in
your quiet breathing as you sleep,
in the song that parts everyone's
trouble, in the moment the old
painter lifts his brush from the
canvas.

Even in these words I leave
on the page like ripples
in the water.

Invisible Mirrors

Things may be named,
but names are not the things.

—Lao Tzu

Invisible
Mirror

It was only a moment,
but the small bird was
gliding at the pace of
the clouds drifting
above us.

It somehow mirrored
the bird of peace gliding
in my heart, waiting for
my confusions to part.

Later that day, I saw a doe
nibbling in the woods, as
the sun spilled across its
neck.

This somehow mirrored
the mind inside my mind
that nibbles at the silence
growing like a weed under
all that I know.

Point of Magic

Nothing in nature asks how to grow.
The flower simply follows the light.
The bear simply forages and becomes
majestic. The dolphin breaches till it
assumes its length. But there's this
point of magic where the soul asks,
"What do you want to be?" And so,
we try on many things, unsure which
will bring us alive. This gateway—before
what we feel comes out of our mouth,
before what we think slips into our
hands—this is what makes the human
journey so spectacular and confusing.

Elemental

The mountains take eons to form.
They hold steadfast to the sky, only
to avalanche in a second, losing the
weaker side of their face.

Under the avalanche, some small
thing stubbornly grows. And it all
begins again.

This is a good way to understand
the build and crash.

When steadfast, anything is possible.
When under the avalanche, all is hell.
When stubbornly growing,
the thing breaking ground
is a miracle, every time.

In the Seams

The young dream of what will be,
while the old chase what has been.

But the heroes are the quiet ones
who listen beyond all they've been
taught: to welcome a circle into
our square, to welcome water
when we've only known fire.

Wisdom comes from those
who can name a thing without
killing it.

Beneath the Trance

In the beginning, we grow toward
truth and love, like plants to the sun,
no shape in mind at all, our mouths
just opening like blossoms.

But somewhere along the way,
truth becomes the metal we forge,
while love becomes the hammer,
as we pound the life out of
what can save us.

Why didn't anyone tell us that
juggling with stars can cut our
hands with light?

A Fine Powder
Covers the Earth

As light causes a flower to open,
deep listening causes the heart
to open.

It is this flowering
that pollinates the world.

To Glide

They say butterflies are born
knowing how to continue their
migration. We have this deep
knowing, too, though we refuse
it when afraid.

Yet after a life of why and how,
we slip into our next incarnation,
becoming each other. This is why
I recognize you when we meet.

They say when eagles fly high
enough, they think of nothing
and trust. If we could only
reclaim this birthright.

Inside Light

Each time all is forgotten,
a night will pass, beyond
which all will be remembered.
I seek the Center because
I want no part of the forgetting.

And so I try, despite the looks of
others, to understand the language
of the Center, in hopes that, as I
come alive, you, unsure of where
you journey, will stop and realize
that our roots tangle somewhere
out of view.

And where we join, there is no
word for why, only how. No
word for Godlike, only God.
No word for mine, only what
is. No word for fear, only
looking again.

Tautologies

When a bird sleeps,
it dreams of flying.

When the heart sleeps,
it dreams of loving.

When the mind sleeps,
it dreams of seeing freshly.

When awake—flying, loving,
and seeing are the same.

Suggestions

When holding on to
whoever is falling,
the molecules of
love fuse.

When letting our light
fill each other's dark,
despair dissipates.

When quiet, we enter
the great stillness at the
Center of All Things, like
bubbles about to surface.

Emptied

When I finally stop, the noise of
my fears and worries leaves my
mind like bees scattering from
a hive.

Once clear, the moments of love
and suffering I've known carry me
in a slow river of being.

And emptied of my life, I start to
receive the currents of others: nearby,
around the world, throughout history.

Until like the stone at the bottom of
a waterfall, I am rounded by the rush
of life.

Suchness

I can endure what breaks, for
I have felt the onset of paradise
and it is not a place we arrive at.

It is not something we put on
like clothes. It pulses beneath
our skin.

I can even endure the dreams
that never grow, for each unlaces
me with what I can't deny—that
life wants only to live, the way
heat wants only to warm.

Radiant

Having pinned the night
with their light one more
time, the stars lie down to
rest as the sun takes over.

Then we wake, to share
what can be eaten and
compost the rest.

And life draws everything
to it, slowly and by starts.

What we believe in grows
like a root inching deeper.

When I can, I listen like
the wind. And you ask your
questions like an old soul
shining a light into a corner.

COATING THE MOON

We do not work on dreams to interpret them,
but they work on us to change us. What we
have to do . . . is simply . . . befriend them.

—JOSEPHINE EVETTS-SECKER

Chords

Once in a while, the
light floods the empty
café making me want to
stop, the way truth can
reach me through a story
I wasn't ready to hear.

Yet it might take years
for a tool to give the
hand all it knows.

We think it all comes
from us when it is we
who are dropped like
pollen.

Impossible to Say

The depth of the sea causes
the surf to lick the features
off the shore, the way the
depth of all-there-is
rearranges all we know.

So it is impossible to settle
on any one conclusion.
Best to let the eyes and
what they see wash anew.

Prudent to let the tongue
and all it wants to say
crumble like a mound
of sand.

Under all that takes place,
we are meant to let go and
let in. This is how beauty
shows itself.

If we could only put every-
thing down like a tired
mountain and receive.

Everyone Is Melancholy

When I miss New York, like now, I close my
eyes and listen to a soft piano and imagine I am
walking in late April through Washington Square,
crossing Sixth Ave, passing dozens of people strol-
ling at dusk, heading home, heading out, weaving
without effort around each other. I duck into that
narrow jazz club on Tenth, to sit at a small wooden
table with its candle flickering. I'm there early, to
soak up the history of the place. The drums breathe
slowly, waiting for the drummer. The bass leans
against the brick wall, waiting for the bow to
release its truth, and the piano, already in my
head, is listening to the small talk of those who
gather. I watch others sip their drinks, alone,
together. Finally, the old, unknown masters sit
behind their instruments for the thousandth
time. And we are transported to the common
center of everyone's melancholy that flickers
inside each of us like the small candle on my
table. After, we all meander between our end-
less stops enroute to staying alive. Like me now,
a thousand miles from the streets I dream of.

Reach into
That Water

Sometimes, on a clear day,
someone will see God in the
bottom of our lake. And having
their heart opened, they will
reach into our water and
break God's reflection
mirrored in them.

At this point, some will stay
and some will go. This is the
difference between falling
in love and staying in love.

In holding each other,
we break the image of God
that drew us. But what
drew us never breaks.

That Which

The greatest liberation is that which
makes us shed our stubbornness,
the way a weary knight takes off his
armor, only to tremble in the rain.

The greatest teacher is that which
deepens the reach of our living, like
a seed that only flowers in our heart
once we stop searching for its name.

The greatest acceptance is that which
makes us ring true, the way the bell
of an ancient gong quiets all speech.

Stitching

In early spring, a tree bends to
the wind and a bird leaves the
tree and a horse follows the bird.
Then water soaks around a root, the
way healthy cells flood to a wound.

This is the stitch work of the world:
things become strong by joining.

Little else matters. Not the schemes,
the dreams, the reasons, the excuses.

They are just twigs in a nest of
trouble that teaches us to fly.

Otherwise

Enduring love can make a soft
water of the heart, while enduring
trouble can make a diamond of
the mind.

Having been broken and remade
many times, I think we have to
love our way through trouble
and keep softening into clarity.

This is the journey of fire and ice,
to heat up and soften. For love
receives and truth reflects. And
we need both.

Otherwise, we become strange
descendants of Midas, where
everything we touch burns up
or freezes.

To Appear

—A new way of seeing
is always worth the climb.

The love we give floats
to the ground like leaves
in autumn, brilliant but,
in time, nowhere to be
found.

That love becomes
the mulch from which
other life grows, never
knowing what we've been
through to give them
a chance.

In Hand

Our hands are capable
of anything. They build,
break, hold, soothe, and
repair.

And while the mind is so
efficient at taking things
apart, the heart waits for
the mind to fail to put
them back together.

While the mind pulls,
the heart joins. And
the hands do what
they are told.

Below All Names

We often live like shadows,
suffering from stories never
told and songs never sung.

Though, even shadows vanish
with enough light. And truth
remains a perception revealed
by time.

To live a full life, we are called
to participate in everything, while
accepting that we control nothing.

So, with nothing left to say, I
explore the wonder in silence
and try to net the stars with
thoughts of the beginning.

Twigging

Sometimes, the thoughts
that plague me fall like pebbles
off a cliff. I never
hear them land.

And the never-landing
sets me free.

And feeling free, I fly into
the lives of others, beaking
their lessons like twigs I use
to build my nest.

And the twigging
lets me breathe.

Then, when I wait for the
geese to cross the road, I
lose all destination.

And the waiting
unfists my life.

Interrogative

When I truly listen, not just
to the words but to the place
where the words surface like old
fish, something opens between us
that is ancient, from which we
come and to which we go.

This kind of listening, which
requires everything without
doing anything, threads me to
you through the endless center
of our hearts.

Listening this way, all moods
can be endured.

Coating the Moon

A leaf lands on the water and
a fish rises to meet it, as if it has
been looking for just this patch
of cool.

A bird drops a branch and a dog
snatches it and runs, as if that stick
were all it ever hoped to catch.

And I pick up what you drop to give
it to someone else because this is what
we do. Aliveness flows through every
meeting.

The way a flare of sun skips across
the galaxy to coat the moon, only
to cascade as moonlight on its way
to earth, landing on your neck,
where it takes my breath away.

Wellspring

Like an old tree, I have more
spaces in my branches. I sway
more in wind.

If you should lean against my
trunk on a hot day, I'll drop a
story or two that seem to
come out of nowhere.

Perhaps you will return when
you feel harried and out of
sorts.

For old souls are like clearings
on the way, like broken bits of
path that somehow make you
pause.

If blessed, we outlast hardship,
only to become a bend in the
river that is hard to leave.

Waiting for Grace

Last month, it appeared while
wading in a lake as the sun split
the clouds, clearing my mind.

Last week, in a mist of silence,
after an ancient phrase of music
unraveled the knot in my heart.

Yesterday, in the exhaustion that
stopped me in the middle of a run,
where I saw the face under my face
in a puddle.

Today, in the morning light
slipping through our blinds on
your shoulder as you sleep.

Utterly

Like a tiger who climbs
a tree, we aspire beyond
ourselves.

Like a note not wanting
to leave the piano, we want
the softest moments to last.

Like a fish who works to
ride the current, we struggle
only to surrender.

Being utterly ourselves,
we discover our kinship
to everything.

Only When

Only when I bow before you
can I spill my assumptions.

Only when I reach to help
can I drop what I cling to.

Only when I open my mouth
in wonder can awe fly in.

And so, to bow, drop, and
open are the covenants
that teach.

The Quieting

I never meant to break what
we built or drop what we
carried for so long.

And though it's taken decades,
I now sign my name to all I
have gathered and lost.

For acceptance lands in the
center of our being like a drop
of rain that parts the lake.

It is the one note that lingers
in the empty hall.

And humility is letting that
one note ring through all
our mistakes.

At Last

I carry less and less
but what I hold is as
singular as a heartbeat.

I know less and less
but what I am certain of
is as constant as light.

I have less and less to say
but what I bear witness to
is as irrevocable as the axis
on which the Earth turns.

To Land Wildly

Welcome to the brink of everything! It takes a lifetime to get here, but the view and the bracing breeze in your face make it worth the trip.

—Parker J. Palmer

A Thousand Dawns

How many lifetimes has my heart
made me reach into the world?

And though I've been hurt, the
endless reaching has made me
stronger.

I used to think I was reaching
for someone or something. But
that was all to get me here, where
reaching for each other is how the
biology of grace keeps us alive.

And what comes to me from
others, glorious others, has always
been more than I've been able to
give, the way a fire grows for
whatever it meets.

To Land Wildly

In time, without knowing, our
want for more is worn like the crags
of a cliff effaced by the sea. Eventually,
suffering wears us down, while love
brings us to the surface and we meet
at the flashpoint of all that is real, no
longer able to hide. Now, everything
is irreducible. Though we look for it
everywhere, we enter the treasure
more than find it, winded to land
right where we are.

A Slow Arrival

Some musicians return to the same
chord and their heart says there's
nowhere else to go. As some painters
can only paint one color. And a scholar,
intent on reading everything, became a
sage when he stumbled into a passage
he could not leave. And so, we search
through loves and adventures, looking
for the one passage in which our soul
can nest and never leave. This is how
humans migrate. We try on everything,
only to end up as we were born—naked.

The Return

We start out so innocent
and then we get hurt. It
doesn't matter how.

What makes things worse
is that we try to get out
of here, to run, to even
disappear.

Of course, none of that
works. Any more than
a bird can escape the sky.

We might even spend
a decade or two hiding
in a cloud.

But the light will find us
and disperse the cloud
around our head,
around our heart.

When this happens,
we think it is another
pain come to undo us.

But it is the freefall
that will send us back
to earth where the
thousand blessings
wait.

What We
Lean On

The seed is inedible
but we need its fruit.

The sun untouchable
but we need its light.

The flood undrinkable
but our roots need its
water.

And the world of sleep
unknowable but we
still need its rest.

Our depth of thought
and feeling is like the
pole a ferryman uses
to cross a river.

We can't see what it
touches way down,
though it steadies
us as we go.

The One
Great Taste

In time, we wander away
from the crowd, down a rocky
path, to the bottom of a ravine
where the sun is relentless on
the patch of stream hardest to
reach. It is there—after love and
loss, after dream and ruin—that
we finally kneel, when no one is
looking, to drink from the ages.

The Ledge

Like a seer in need of
horizons, I've spent my
life looking into these
spaces, sitting on the
edge of every cliff,
peering into the sea.

What I bring back
are the poems.

At first, I was thrilled to
witness anything. Then,
it was uplifting to open
the poems like windows, so
you could be dizzied, too.

Now, I want to bring you
there and dive into the
horizon together.

Tikkun Olam

Have I repaired the bench
we brought from Albany
one too many times?

It sways when I sit on it.
Am I just being stubborn?

Yet, we repair our love,
no matter how we sway.

We keep upgrading
our glasses. Keep changing
our frames. Shouldn't we
repair the Truth?

Isn't the world one endless
bin of parts aching to be
put back together?

Like you. Like me. Like
the stars, which, having
drifted too far apart, call
to us in our sleep, to make
a constellation of them.

The Feel of Other Life

How you and I, like ordinary heroes,
are tethered to all the other living
things, known to each other and
not. When one of us falls, some
pull near. When one of us flies,
others are lifted. Sure, trouble will
knot our strings for a while. But
nothing will cut us loose. Not
even death.

The Ship of Theseus

It was Heraclitus who asked, if a
ship has been thoroughly rebuilt—
new sails, new mast, new hull—
is it still the same boat?

And if a soul is remade, is
it still the same soul?

Or when a mind has its
assumptions cracked open,
is it still the same mind?

If you believe in the Gravity
of Spirit, nothing is lost.

After all, the body replaces all
its cells every seven years and
we remain who we are.

This is how I recognize the flare
of what's Eternal as it coats your
suffered voice.

How a cinder carries the image
of all it has burned. How the
heart carries the taste
of all it has loved.

Giving It Away

Each time we suffer or love,
we are dipped like a ladle into
the waters that outlive us.

Like a ladle that is emptied
before each scoop, we know
loss before fullness.

Like a ladle, filled to pour,
we overflow so others may
drink from all we've been
through.

And being emptied
only to be immersed
only to be drunk from
is the fate of an
awakened soul.

Dad

You've been gone eight years
and this time of day you appear
on these late fall mornings in the
light through the oak. I imagine
you hammering on a project that
never ends somewhere near the
sun with all the wood and nails
you could ever want. Now the light
of you spills on your tools which I
keep on my desk: the calipers, the
red-handled awl, the small T-square.
I sit here, drifting between what
you held and where you've gone.
Oh, let's talk now that you've left
your shell of stubbornness. Craft
is what you gifted me. You built
a boat in our backyard. It took
years. I wonder what you're
building on the other side.

Let's Be Real

I dream of lifting the hood from
your eyes and you dream of doing
the same for me.

Better to admit that we are each
blind in a particular way, which
is why we need each other.

Don't point out that I am lame.
Just offer your one good leg, so
that together we can walk.

Looking After

Embrace it and it endures.
Forsake it and it dies.

—Confucius

Stop watering the plants and they
will wither. Stop feeding the dog
and she will start snapping.

Stop watering your mind and it
will wilt. Stop feeding your heart
and you will find fault with
everything.

Pour care on all you meet and
you will be part of a waterfall
that never ends.

Receive care from all you meet
and you will be part of a garden
that will harvest itself.

The Work of Time

In time, what matters is carried
in the smallest part: in a pigeon's
feather, frozen in the crack of a
winter wall, which thaws in spring,
to be found by a child who brings
it home because it means that
anything is possible.

Years later, the child becomes a
dancer and has the feather put in
a locket to remind her why she
dances. In time, she places it on
her daughter's bed stand.

The line between what we lose
and gain is ever effaced, the way
the line between life and death
begins to blur, the more we are
carried to the mouth of the sea.

At Your Table

When I stopped and listened
to the woman born in a man's
body, I understood that everyone
is nectar inside a different flower.

And there was the burn survivor
barely recognizable but all aglow
within. And the vet back from
Afghanistan, unable to sleep.

Everyone has their rise and fall.
In the well we call heart, we are
all the same.

Three Ripples

Sometimes, love can calm us,
the way a sudden wind can lift
the leaves of worry so the light
can reach our trunk.

And sometimes, mercy can
arrive like snow on our lashes,
softening all we see.

And truth can arrive like a drop
of rain on a lake, remaking
our clarity.

There All Along

When young, we shared what
we gathered. Now, we share
what we've lost.

And having tossed what I've
carried, I now want it back and
look for it in the woods, only
to be stopped by the empty
space in a patch of leaves.

Now, the moon sends its light
into the space between the leaves,
stirring me with this want for
tomorrow.

Taken from the Nest

Since stepping out of the first cave, we have made pilgrimage, trying to find where we are going by opening our hearts to where we began. Yet how can any of us tell where the other has been? You, ahead of me in the checkout line, what have you lost and gained along the way that I will never know? They say the great flamingos of India prefer to migrate in a cloudless sky. They can travel up to four hundred miles a night and when they land, who can know what they have seen? We all prefer to find our way at night when no one is looking. Like old owls, we bump into each other and squint. And the great savannah elephants of Africa migrate for the scent of a den no longer there. Like you or me making pilgrimage through our years of dream and grief. Perhaps our entire time on Earth is just a migration between the wonder of beginning and the effort to carry that wonder to the end.

Praying I Will Find

I used to have so many plans, good plans,
grand plans. In the beginning, I would be
annoyed by the calamities I'd meet along
the way that would keep me from my plans.

I used to pride myself on how I could get
back on track so quickly. But the more I
loved and the more I suffered, the more
my plans were interrupted by those in
need.

Eventually, the call of life, unexpected
and unrehearsed, made swiss cheese of
my plans.

Now, like an emperor undressed by time,
I wander the days naked of plans, praying
that I will find love to give and suffering
to heal before the sun goes down.

What We Leave

By the time you read this,
I will have come and gone,
but the words will point
to what you need.

By the time you look in
earnest, what I have learned
will comet across the sky,
giving off enough light for
you to see for yourself.

By the time you follow
what matters, my life will
have meteored into a pebble
that you will hold like a
rosary, to help you know
which way to go.

Book Two

THE GODS VISIT

If you're going to see the spaces in the leaves,
you have to paint the leaves first.

—MN

The Strength To Go On

In my poetry, as in my teaching, my hope is that people will come away knowing their own gifts and wisdom more deeply; that my poetry, especially, can serve as a window to the vastness of life and the unbreakable Center of all that keeps us alive. My hope is that each poem and each teaching moment can restore our direct kinship with all living things.

If we keep taking off our assumptions and conclusions, like clothes, we return to the innocence we were born with, before we were named, before we had any sense of time passing or any sense of dreams to be lived into. For at birth, time and dream are one. And we gather and empty many times over a lifetime to recover that feeling of being born. This is one of the transforming purposes of poetry, to return us to the freshness of birth, again and again.

Despite the race of our days, there is a soft rhythm that runs under everything, like a breeze below trouble. Though we'd like to live there, we can't escape the weather of the world. We can only find and refind that rhythm to soften the journey. This is a practice all its own: how to soften all that is jarring, not running from life but learning to settle more deeply into what we are given. This is one of the anchoring purposes of poetry, to settle us more deeply into what is.

And every time the ineffable shows itself—like light through clouds or wind through trees—the gods, so old they have lost their names, visit us, to give us strength to go on. These poems, written in my seventieth year, bear witness to this life-giving mystery.

Under the Temple

I know there is no straight road,
no straight road in this world.
Only a giant labyrinth
of intersecting crossroads.

—Federico García Lorca

Metamorphosis

While sitting in a waiting room
for my chemo, the young mother
next to me took my arm and uttered,
"I'm not ready to die." I squeezed
her hand and we both welled up.

That was thirty years ago and though
I don't know what happened to her,
I have been carried all this time like
a small flower on a fast stream.

Since then, I have seen how nothing
in life is untouched. Storms break
trees and spring lets them grow into
two trees. And the heart, breaking,
keeps growing, larger and softer.

I confess, I don't know how any
of this happens. Only that even
gray days like today are beautiful
in the depth of their grayness.

Somehow, under all our struggles,
the spaces within are bare, not
empty, like the hollow of a lute
waiting for life to strum us until
our music can be played.

Under the Temple

The temple hanging over the water is
anchored on pillars that nameless workers
placed in the mud long ago. So never forget
that the mud and the hands of those workers
are part of the temple, too. What frames the
sacred is just as sacred. The dirt that packs
the plant is the beginning of beauty. And
those who haul the piano on stage are the
beginning of music. And those who are
stuck, though they dream of soaring,
are the ancestors of our wings.

The Wall Builder

I knew a man so hurt by love,
he created a tower of require-
ments to try again.

And the poet H.D. made the
hole through which her poems
could pass so small and perfect
that she erased her whole life's
work.

I used to long for what was
unreachable, frustrated at what
I couldn't express.

But having too many preferences
is how we build a wall so high
that no one can climb it or so
clear that no one can find it.
Then, we wonder why we are
so lonely.

And blaming everyone for our
loneliness is just another
kind of wall.

Swordless

They say the old samurai,
tired of being on guard, gave
his sword away.

It took months to accept a life
without armor, months to let his
wounds turn into blossoms.

In time, he took to long walks
along the river where he would
sit alone and play the one-stringed
koto.

Sought out by a young soldier, the
former hero listened into dusk and
simply said, "I have looked my whole
life for the one string."

When the would-be warrior asked
about greatness, the swordless samurai
replied, "Understanding life is like toss-
ing a scarf in the air and watching
it drape its way to the ground."

Never Lost,
Always Found

On the darkest night of the year,
Susan asks about Grandma Minnie
yet again. And again, I soften and speak
of being a child in your Brooklyn kitchen,
sitting next to your stove as you made
latkes, patting the excess oil and giving
them to me while they were warm.

And Susan jumps up, as she does every
year, as if for the first time, and starts
grating potatoes. I put on klezmer music
and we make latkes and eat standing
in the kitchen.

Our dog jumps to the music or to
the presence of something unseen.
I grab her paws and we dance briefly
to the music of the old world.

I Behold Each

These days, I wander in the forest
of retrievable truths. One appeared
as an old fish staring up through a pool.
Another as a dragon asleep in a cloud.
And this one was waiting in a throw
of pine needles scattered by the hoof
of a small deer.

Each stops me with its wonder or
its weight until I listen with my
whole being.

But nothing can be taken from
this wilderness. And so, I behold
each with an image or two that I
tuck in my heart.

When I return, I drop them on
the page. When I show it to you,
we both go quiet and call it a poem.

The Mute Sage

When the jar fell off the counter
and broke, our dog went to lick up
the honey but we were afraid she'd
cut herself on the broken glass.

You kept her back while I swept
up the slivers. Later that night,
it occurred to me that this is
what it is to be human: always
going for the honey while
tiptoeing around the glass.

The next week, it was so cold
that ice stuck to our dog's pads.
We had to stop every block or so
to free her feet from clumps of ice.
This too was a lesson. For without
warmth, we cannot make our way.

As I write this, she dreams whatever
dogs dream and I keep looking for
whatever humans look for.

So She Could

Overwhelmed by all the deadlines,
she stopped the clocks in her house
and buried her watch in the garden,
so she could feel the slower time that
trees obey.

And broken by the relentless news,
she unplugged her devices, so she could
listen for how things come together, the
way streams join rivers which then join
the sea.

Burdened by her past, she burned all
the letters and gave away the keepsakes,
so she could stop reliving her story.

Have We

Now that the bills are paid and
the oil in the car has been changed,
and the dishes are done, now that
the song we both love has played,
now that we have unraveled our
thoughts like yarn on the floor,
tell me, have we walked by what
matters one too many times?

Have we let our pain distract us
more than work us through? Can
we clean the gutters of our past
and let the rains swell our roots?

For all the hours crossed like miles,
have we let our souls pour into
the world enough?

Finding Our Way

A cramp of conscience can bring
us to our knees, and a grip of pain
can keep us from our true nature.

Yet as one bit of color can bring the
eye to the center of a painting, one
bit of truth can restart the heart.

Without Interference

The river is not forced.
It simply flows to the sea.
And the wind is not ordered to
slip through the canyon. Nor the
light conscripted or shamed into
filling every crack. Nor are we
forced to care. Given time, the
truth boils and kindness brews.
And the eyes, once softened,
see through every covering.

Being True

I thought it was my efforts
in being true that made me
somewhat wise, but I woke
today aware of those who have
loved me, feeling the warmth
of their tea.

And looking back from this
plateau, which some call accept-
ance, I can see that each polished
a facet of my heart, each
made me see-through.

It is being held through
the storm that makes us a gem.

The Art
of Grounding

Starting out, I needed someone
or something to bring the love
out of me. But falling through,
love is now like air.

Now, rather than coming alive
through those I love, I let life
flow through me to everything
and everyone.

Now, when I touch you, I am
a lightning rod giving back.

If Endured

When things break, it's natural
to sort through all that is lost, but
essential to look for the one piece
under the rubble that didn't break.

Crucial to pick it up and hold it
close like an ancient horn a Shaman
blows to make his troubles sleep.

Oh, there is no escaping the loss,
which will lead us and rearrange us.

But under all the ash is the one
bone that will not burn.

You Taught Me

When I was lost, you came and
rubbed my shoulders till my judg-
ment of myself dispersed.

When I was too heavy with grief
to fold the laundry, you said, "Forget
the dryer" and hung the clothes on
the line and we watched the shirts
and sheets billow in the wind.

When I was ready to give up, you
bought me a small drum whose
deep red tone helped me re-hear
the Center of Things.

Now you are broken and sad and
I am busy finding things for you
because you taught me that it's
the giving back and forth that
saves us.

Like mouth-to-mouth
resuscitation, we pass the breath
of life from the one who is lit
to the one who is not.

THE ANCIENT DRIFT

Think of this One Original Source as a spring,
self-generating, feeding all of itself to the rivers
and yet not used up by them, ever at rest.

—PLOTINUS

Octaves Apart

At times, like now, there is the
inexplicable sensation that as I
write from the depths of my heart,
which is so unique to me, I am also
touching into the timeless well of
all feeling. And so, the echoing sense
that others write these words in their
own way at the same time. Like a
trembling hand dipped into a
clear lake, what I thought
was mine is everyone's.

Almost

As I push this empty boat from
the dock, I am certain there is a
drift under everything: opening the
throat of a bird, pumping the heart
in its want to join, and lifting the
belly of a whale.

It's in a quiet turn at the bottom
of the sea, in the patch of calm
inside every trouble.

Below all the noise, I can almost
feel the Earth drifting in place.
Then, I wonder, what barely per-
ceivable nudge set the Universe in
motion? Out of what beautiful nothing
did all this shy magnificence emerge?

Sketching in Air

He always talked the way he
sketched, in large, free circles
that never seemed to meet. And
just as his paintings loosened over
the years—from still life to impres-
sions to abstract vibrations—his
stories unlaced into their primary
colors with no beginning, middle,
or end. Now, on soft winter days,
it's enough just to listen to him
the way you might listen to
an ancient waterfall.

In Your Hand

I know you can only see red right now
through the cut in your trust. But most
cuts mend and then, the courage is in
finding an open boat so you can row
far enough out that you can drift.

And only when you have given up
going anywhere might you be drawn
to pick up the oars and start rowing
at the pace of clouds.

Then, as your hand is one with the oar
and the oar is one with the water, your
heart will be one with your life and
your life will be one with the ancient
drift that joins all things.

Wingspan

When the mind stops,
the heart eases. Then my
soul hovers, the way a hawk
glides, watching everything.

In these moments, I never
want to land or pump my
wings again. This might be
joy, letting life carry us.

This might be peace, moving
without moving, the mind
and heart ever opening.

Inscapes

Out in the world, I follow slim
waves from the overlook, watch
snow land on the mountain half-
way up, and look long into the
canyon from the creaky bridge.

But in here, a regret is tossed
like a pebble into the waterfall
of changes, and I look into the
basin of light from which we
come and return.

In here, if I hike far enough, I
forget how to speak as when I'm
at the cabin by the lake for weeks.

Though it took years to find,
there is an inner cabin where
I walk beside words.

For the song I would voice
has already gone into the
world and back.

For Tu Fu

It was the spirit of Tu Fu from
the Tang Dynasty who gave me
strength to endure my cancer.
Now, years later, he appears again,
in a book of translations, each carried
like a pail of water across the centuries.
This time he laments how the autumn
storms tore thatches from his roof and
he woke to see patches of straw fly into
the river. In the morning, he could see
parts of his roof tangled in the trees.
If not for the cold, he would have
preferred sleeping under the sky.
On the page above his poem
is a print by Han Gan of sixteen
horses in various poses. If I could,
I'd tie a poem to the saddle of each
and send them back to the great one
who didn't know he was great, to
let him know that the red shock
of his heart still lives on.

This Takes Time

What you drop, I pick up.
We don't even have to be
in the same place to benefit
each other.

As an apple draws life from
the sun before it lands in the
mouth of a skinny deer,

the Unnamable Spirit sets
the laughter of a child in the
path of someone's misfortune.

They say when painters squint,
the threads of light become
more visible. Just so.

As we let go our definitions,
what holds the Universe
together shows itself.

How Dust Settles

Without knowing you, I pause
and stare into the quiet between
tall buildings, and you do the same
as you stir your tea, and the woman
opening the post office drops her keys
and sighs to be here at all. And the
longing we each have to be rid of all
the anger and discourse forms a breeze
that stops a dozen more souls. This,
too, is how God moves among the
discontented.

Before

Before a bird can fly, it falls.
Before a fish can swim, it sinks.
Before we can say yes to life, we
sputter and hesitate.

Everything that matters is brought
into the open by this give and take.

For before a fire flares, the wood
must burn. And before we can
see the shimmer of what is, we
must burn what we want.

Too often, the things we wear
as failure are just the physics
of grace.

Between Sparks

—In the midst of all the hiding,
I want you to see through me.

I don't want anything from you,
only the spark that lights us both
when we truly touch. Come, land
under my shade the way a moth
hovers near a lamp.

For something in being this
close makes us stop fluttering.

Something enters when we
hold nothing back that is more
life-giving than anything
we can save or hoard.

Mysteriously

You can catch a firefly in a
jar, but you can't hold light.

And you can watch an idea
flit about the jar of your mind,
but you can't hold thought.

As light from the sun travels
93 million miles, invisibly,
only seen the instant it touches
this broken twig, Spirit travels
unseen, across the ages, till it
flares the tip of your heart.

From This Cliff

I can see the sailboats below being
carried across the bay, always from
west to east, no matter how they
zig and zag.

The way that time carries us from
birth to death, no matter our plans.

From here, it is comforting to see
how the sails stay full and how the
water always parts for us.

Off Course

Once, I heard an angel.
She nudged me with a breeze.
I turned and saw a limb sway
and knew the two were one.
Ever since, I tend to roam.

INSIDE THE MUSIC BOX

To live a spiritual life we must first find the courage to enter into the desert of our loneliness and to change it by gentle and persistent efforts into a garden of solitude.

—HENRI NOUWEN

Inside the Music Box

The music box the sad one buried
carries his sadness like a fume into the
head of the one who unearths it. And the
shovel a young couple used to plant their
first garden softens the hand of a miser
who buys it years later at a garage sale.
The honest things we reveal when no
one is watching linger in the air, urging
strangers to be honest. It's impossible
to know what's mine and what's yours.
Like wood split from different trees,
we all burn in the same fire.

The Dead Poet
to the Young One

I hover over a college student
lost in the forest of his mind, one
of my books on his lap. He is caught
in the metaphor I found that changed
everything. He reads it over and over,
as if I authored it. He shows it to a
friend who doesn't understand, who
wants him to go for a beer. He leaves
me in his knapsack, but his heart keeps
circling the metaphor. He lags behind
and goes silent. Up here, we don't speak.
We just pass through people, like wind
through fields, to draw everything into
the One. Unsure what is calling, he
drinks too much, then slows to find
me in a corner of the sky.

Yet to Break

When we first arrive, it
seems the sky will show us
how the earth will hold
us when we weep.

But we have yet to love
or betray one another.
We have yet to hold onto
something that will break.

And of all those I could
have leaned on when broken,
there was you. Because of you,
I learned to trade the storm
for the depth.

In truth, any of us could slip
in this instant into the well
of all there is and disappear.

That is, we might love so
fully that we will become
part of the thing well loved.

Like a wave in the middle
of the night resuscitating
the shore.

From the Beginning

I can listen to these few
measures of piano over and
over. Each coaxes the stone
from the mouth of my heart.
Why look for something extra
or different? It's always about
finding the One Chord and living
with it. It's the same with love.
We don't need someone special
or new. We need the original oar
of feeling to part us like water
again and again. Some are open-
ed by the sweep of birds crossing
the sky. Some are softened by
watching their dogs sleep. And
some like me are stalled on the
cliff of each moment, brought
alive by a vastness that
humbles and pulls.

Arpeggio

Missing you, I leave a note
at your door, never knowing that
the wind blows it on the porch of
the widow next door. And reading
my confession, the old woman relives
her own journey of becoming known.
It makes her fill the feeders and the
robins, happy to be fed, sing a lighter
tune which stops the serious girl in
the middle of her piano lesson.
For how can any practiced phrase
approach the suddenness of song?
At times, it goes like this. The
missing leads to dreaming which
leads to feeding the small things
of the world. At times, we help
each other without ever knowing.

Coming of Age

A young seeker played his flute
under a cypress when a swan ap-
peared. For a moment, it seemed
the swan was dancing to what the
seeker was playing. And he thought,
This must be what it is to be great.

Years later, after much loss and
tragedy, the great one returned,
much gentler. And when the swan's
swan appeared, he played his flute
in response to the bird dancing
on the leaves. And he thought,
This must be what it is to be free.

Toward the end, the old one
returned yet again. Unable to
play, he just held his flute on his
lap and listened to the wind play
him like a song. And resting like
a swan, he thought, *This must be
what it is to be loved.*

I Carry Their Faces

The insecure one says, "You never
listen!" While the sad one says, "I
can't bear anymore!" And the hurt
one looks in anger for something
to break that will equal the break
he feels inside. While the one in
need keeps taking up space as the
humbled one stays out of view, not
to hide, but to lure the secrets of life
into the open. And the blind one sees
more than the rest of us. While the one
who can't stop talking runs right by the
one so full of light. I have been each of
these and carry their faces like facets
of a prism. This is the tumble.

Yellow Requiem

You've both been gone for eight
years and I am turning seventy. I still
miss what we never had. Even when you
were here, I had become my own mother,
my own father. It took some time but I
can remember a beautiful moment in
the eye of the storm that was our life.
It was on a summer night in our small
backyard around a fire as the peepers
grew loud and we all stopped arguing
for a long moment. While you were
staring into the fire, I stared into you.
In that oyster glow, I could part your
anger and see past your wounds, all
the way to the soft center you found
in each other before I was born. Now
I thread these images like beads of truth
on a necklace I call you that strings from
before I was here to who knows where.

For Kenzie

Before we buy tickets, before
we drive and park and fill the
theatre, the dancer all alone closes
her eyes and spins about the Axis
of the Universe with no one watch-
ing until the Dance of Time fills her
arms and her legs. Spinning slowly
like a flower opening, she starts to
glow. And all the practice from that
point on is just to bring that glow
of opening to others. Though it is
called a performance, when the
lights are low and the dance begins,
something is stirred in everyone
that keeps the world going.

Crossroads

When hurt and frightened,
we can push off and fight like
hell or drop everything and
ask for help.

When backed into the corner
of all we know, we can claw
and thrash or turn around
and enter the new world.

Each day is a ledge we
can fall from or a sacred
mountain we can climb.

Rapid Transit

Worn of our preferences,
life is immediate.

Admitting we don't know,
we become touchable.

Exhausted of our differences,
there is room for everyone.

The War Between Us

The one couldn't land and the other
couldn't stop praying to the ground.

For the first ten lifetimes, they found
the other lacking and secretly thought
each other the enemy.

By the time the great fire came and
went, they were exhausted enough
to see the other as their teacher.

After ten more lifetimes, they com-
pleted each other and died as one.

Not What It Seems

We are so busy filling ourselves that we
seldom feel the growth in being emptied.

Yet it is the rest stop in a symphony that
draws everyone to it, and the slot where
a nail used to be that begs to be repaired,
and our innocence of mind like a hole
in a fence that lets us know the world.

As threads need holes to do their job,
it is the interstices of nothing that hold
everything together.

Drag and Sweep

No matter what happens, the love
we have for others never goes away.
Like a bottle of wine spilled on the
ground, you can't put it back.
So where does it go?

I think it keeps the heart moist
as a sponge lifted from the deep,
making me grateful, even to
those who left me.

I think it makes the back of our
eyes glow. I think it stops me from
thinking and softens all the edges
until the drag and sweep of heart
makes us love again.

Led Like an Ox

Each life is a koan to be lived with.
And try as we do to solve each other,
we are led, in time, to take off our
judgments like glasses and eat the
essence of another like a berry
we had no idea was there.

THE ONE RAIN

Perhaps there is a language which is not made of words and everything in the world understands it. Perhaps there is a soul hidden in everything and it can always speak, without even making a sound, to another soul.

—HELEN NEARING

Notice

Imagine a lantern in an open boat,
the light flickering as the boat drifts
in the night lake.

Now imagine it rains and look closely
at how the drops plop in the lake
and thud in the boat and bead on
the sides of the lantern.

Notice how the flame doesn't
go out.

Inside Liberty

I clung to life with the ways
I was taught. It was like gripping
a bird I had to toss to the wind.

It seems we are never closer
than when setting things free.

For only when empty-handed
can life be our teacher.

Now when I rest, I go quiet
like the thousand beings
asleep in the forest.

It's enough to make a star
want to drink from a stream.

Patience

Unable to keep from dispersing,
the long shelf of clouds gives way
to the sun. It is the same with trouble.
We always wake under truth, only
to be covered by clouds, only
to outwait what's in the way.

This is the weather of the mind.

And so, I pray the way I work,
giving my all to outlast winter,
to feel the warmth waiting in
everything.

The Ancient Door

When I ring the chimes,
I follow the sound till it slips
into silence the way a fox slips
through a hole in the brush, and
I am reminded of how I am rung
by the moments that align, the
way wind plays itself out in the
leaves. And the pause that's left
opens the latch to an ancient
door.

Then I fall in without falling.
And give my name away with-
out losing who I am. Then it
all makes sense and I am left
with nothing and everything.

Nowhere To Go

Yesterday, everything seemed
just right. The past, present, and
future aligned briefly and there
was nowhere to go.

This morning, everything has
tightened and I am not where I am.

It's as if the Universe dilates and
constricts around us and we call the
dilation peace, and the constriction
worry.

All the while, my dog sleeps, curled
and safe because of our love.

I long for such moments.

Long After

How do we keep shedding
without disappearing? How does
taking off make us stronger? I just
know that reaching long enough,
we forget what we are reaching
for. Then, we become the beauty
of the gesture. Then, we arc like
deepfelt statues waiting to be
sculpted. When bare and honest,
we send our love into the future
the way stars send their light
long after they have died.

Above the Clouds

Once we break through the canopy,
they tuft and roll in a sea of white,
waves of air lifting and crashing so
slowly they seem to hide the most
forgotten gods: the one who
loves us anyway, the one who
turns our prayers into dreams,
the one who keeps us looking
to the sky for what is needed
to see the light in each other.
Back on the ground, Heaven
grows underfoot like a weed.

Astonishing

that waterfalls never end, that
droplets fall from the sky coaxing
wood to grow out of the ground,
that the pebble in your shoe makes
you stop in time to see the eagle
spread its wings, that the song in
our heart leaves our mouth the
way a bird leaves its nest, that
truth crosses the mind the way
light comes and goes in an alley,
that all I ever wanted is in the
bit of being left like broken glass
between us, that each life is just
a match lit in the cave of time.

White Leaves

After our argument, I sputtered
to anyone who would listen. After
that, I stewed inside till I grew tired
of my turbulence. Finally, like a table-
cloth snapped and floating above
its table, I settled into myself.

That winter, after the first snow,
the air was especially still and I
thought of you as our dog plowed
her nose through the white leaves.

Missing you, I stopped to stare at
the bend in a tree that no one notices
until its arguments are covered.

To Suffer the Wait

As the wind fills a sail waiting for
direction, the will, surrendered,
waits to be instructed.

Though it seems like we are doing
nothing, it requires courage
not to proclaim a cause
where there is none.

Better to teach a young one to
look in the places we seldom look.

Let Us Learn Together

Leave a cup out in the rain and you
will know the fate of an open mind.

Fill a bird feeder to the brim and you
will know the gift of an open heart.

Let the corn grow sweet under its husk
and you will taste the heart of all wisdom.

Revealed in Winter

It takes the cooling of the Earth
and the shedding of all these leaves
so that in December, when the sun
comes up, it will pierce through the
armless limbs. And this bare moment,
despite the cold, affirms how Spirit
shines through whatever we grow in
the way, like truth through the thicket
of denial or humility through the
briars of arrogance. Now a light
snow falls on everything that is
struggling to survive.

Winds We Can't See

When the thief died, he came back
as a blind dragon and after a life of
fire and chaos, the dragon came back
as a peony too heavy in its beauty to
keep its head up. And having withered,
the peony came back as a broken shell
washed ashore. Now, after years of being
tucked in the sand, the shell comes back
as a young woman who struggles her
whole life with who to listen to: the
thief and the dragon or the beauty
growing in her shell.

The One Rain

I am sitting on a screened–in porch
watching the rain pummel the lake,
each drop rippling into the other.

Somehow, moments of true feeling
fall like rain into the lake of time
until we can't resist becoming
each other.

Our loves and losses keep merging,
impossible to keep your pain from
my joy or my worry from your
calm.

Try as we do, each time we fall,
the heart of your life is my life.
The smell of water is everywhere.

CLOSE TO FINDING
OUR PLACE

*The soul is . . . the center of all things . . .
it passes into all things . . . it is the true
connection of all things . . . it goes to the one
without leaving the other . . .*

—MARSILIO FACINO

Beyond Asking

The mind stirs like a hive
eager to make its honey.

But on a day like today, after
decades of trying too hard,
as the sun releases the truth
of what's already made,

the only thought I have drifts
like a cinder or snowflake or
an asterisk close to finding
its place.

Whether

Lincoln said a person is
responsible for their face
after forty. If we smile
when no one is looking,
our face will bloom.
If we sneer when at rest,
our face will crumble.

Likewise, if we grumble
at every turn, we will tight-
en into no. If we face what
befalls us, we will widen
into yes.

This is not about putting
on a happy face or refram-
ing what is difficult.

This is about whether
we fight the fall into life
or dive.

A Patch of Night

The sun casts its light across the
galaxy reflecting off the almost-full
moon and on through a streak of night
clouds, lighting them within, and that
gossamer of night lights your face as we
step into the cold looking up. In just this
way, everything is connected. When some-
one falls, it makes us bend. When someone
grows, it helps us find the strength to get
off our knees. I trace the light on your face
to the moonlit cloud to the moon and
back to the Source I can't yet see.

All We Can Do

The same sweep of arm that swings
the scythe lowers the sword and paints
the world. The same reach that twirls the
dance skips the stone of truth across the
lake. And the same leap through fire to
save another crosses the chasm of lone-
liness to make a friend. Yes, the same
hand that docks a weary life catches
what has fallen. We never know what
will lift or crash. All we can do is vow
to stay close, to stop the bleeding when
we bleed, and sing each other to sleep
or awake, whichever will soothe us
into tomorrow.

To Another

Watching my wife feed a
chickadee, I suddenly see
that life is an infinite chain
of one form freeing another.

We wake from our suffering
to realize our only purpose
is to free the bird in the cage
before us.

Then we find ourselves in a
cage and wait for another
to wake and free us.

This goes on and on until
the tree frees the bird and
the sky frees the tree and
the sun frees the sky.

Every day, it starts all over.
Being part of this, my
wife begins to glow.

Ever Toward

Let me get up when I'm down
and open when I'm closed.

Let me give one more time than
I think possible and receive one
more time than I resist.

Let me stop trying to delineate
life and keep trying to release it.

Let me find agreement with all
I don't understand

so I can stay as brave as the tops
of trees that never stop reaching
for the sky

and accepting as the kelp along
the ocean floor that lives
to bend with the current.

The Ride

A fish we-didn't-know-was-there
thrashes at the surface and disappears.
It takes time for the water to clear.

Old feelings of those not loved well
are such fish. Being alive is to be
such a lake: accepting what rises
and waiting for the heart to clear.

When still as that water, we
reflect the stars.

This is the ride of being human:
feeling all that is in us so we can
receive all that is beyond us.

A Kind of Baffle

As that squirrel lives to climb the feeder,
no matter what kind of baffle we put up,
the mind wants to solve every problem. This
can be helpful until we need to undress the
stubborn want that sees everything as a
problem. Then something akin to water
is needed, something that will teach us how
to receive, the way the very planet receives
the long, endless pull of the sun, ever lead-
ing us through the weary grip of night.

On Any Given Day

Two cells join to heal a cut,
while halves of a worm grow into
two worms, as a family of deer dart
across the highway at the moment
two strangers meet in a café, and
halfway around the world, two
bodies of water wear away the inlet
between them, while up the coast,
an avalanche forms a bridge be-
tween two peaks, and on a day
like today, thousands of planes
buzz through soft clouds that rim
the planet, each carrying earthbound
souls, some wondering where they
are going and why.

Unexpected

The lost one said, "I need your eyes.
The ones I have can barely see."

The lonely one answered, "I need
your hands, for the ones I have can
barely feel."

And the one stuck in denial finally
admitted, "I need to accept where I
am, for I can't find what matters."

They tossed their insufficiencies into
the fire and in the truth that flared,
they slowly became themselves.

In the morning that followed,
anarchy withered.

If We Are To Live

So much is done to run from death.
But this is not the same as opening to life.
For to put down the sword is not yet the
effort to heal. And to retreat into silence
is not yet the tremble to repair.

There is this antechamber between living
and not living that we decompress in, the
way a diver acclimates when coming back
to the surface. But this in between is not
our home. And courage, the kind that no
one will ever notice, asks that we shed our
apparatus and break for air with a gasp.

Rearranged

When seeing ourselves in
everything, life becomes a
broken mirror and nothing
is possible.

So let the ocean of experience
wash away everything that's
in your grip.

Until all you have planned
is rearranged like a trail in
sand washed clean by the
surf.

Under Our Concerns

No matter the color of our dream,
we tumble through time, sputtering
when we fall, grateful when we land.

On the way, we think we're in control
until a great wave cracks the wheel.
Then we pray to be carried safely.

Then, there's something holy in just
putting our face in the sun.

Under all our concerns, each day slips
by, like a truth dropped in a well, a rough
jewel we can't go after and can't get back.

The New Year

One more time from grief to
humility, like the moon that
hides its face, only to return.

One more time putting down
what we're taught and seeking
more of what songbirds dream.

One more time around.
One more time from in to out.
One more time wanting less.

THE BOTTOM
OF HEAVEN

Let's imagine ourselves
as astronauts of our
very own becoming—
as we're thrown
against the stars.

—ROBERT MASON

Some Say

You can climb to the top
of Machu Picchu and the
bottom of Heaven will fill
your lungs.

Or you can seek out the
shaman on the east coast
of China who soaks a tiger
bone in rice for a broth
that will keep you strong.

And some say, if you just
stay true to all you hold
dear, what matters will
clear your eyes, wherever
you are.

Remnant

I found my grandmother's steamship ticket
to this country from 1904 in the back of her
dresser. And when my father died, there was
a heavy pair of pliers in his old box of tools
in the basement. These are remembrances of
what is needed to leave and what is needed
to stay. Just what will you find of mine and
what will it remind you of? I leave these odd
voicings along the way with no intent other
than to affirm that life is worth living and
that all we have is now and each other.
These are tools unto themselves.

Great Pauses

The old painter is getting a
pacemaker today. His heart has
these great pauses when everything
stops. There are medical reasons but
his whole life he's been stopped by
awe, gasping at the widening miracle
which dizzies him beyond words into
colors and shapes and even into the
undressing of shapes. Is it any wonder
that he endures great pauses? It's there
that he sees beyond the Veil of the Uni-
verse, always returning with a joy he
can't express. Often, when I call, he
is close to tears, listening to some
wave of classical music, the way I
am close to tears listening to him.

The Days Become

In the beginning, it is about facing life
which calls us to open everything with
our mind which is the path, at times,
to our heart.

But somewhere along the way, it is
about facing death which calls us back
to the formless reservoir from which
we are made.

Then, the days become a rickety
wooden bridge. And with every step,
the entire journey teeters as we hold
onto each other, made breathless
by the view.

In Time

After all we reach for and all
we run from, the things that
last start to sing their way
into our hands.

In time, our care sticks to
everything and we start
to glow.

Even when lost, we glide
like birds of light floating
through time.

A History
of Clouds

The old samurai
turned poet said
that once his barn
burned to the ground,
he could see the moon
more completely.

As those around me
burn, I too can see
all the way to the
Beginning.

It makes this life
a barn full of holes
that gives way to
the sky.

One day, one of us
will crumble like a
statue no longer able
to hold its pose.

Though this feels
tragic, it is, in the
end, a revelation.

Doorways

The call is not to leave this
life by falling into the canyon
of a lover's eye or to chase the
highest summit or even to fall
through a poem to another
time.

The call is to go through every
doorway and come back.

The way you might take off
your clothes to bathe in the
lake on the far side of the trail
before heading home.

We must face and honor our
journey and then take off all
we've been through so we can
bathe in life without all that
has happened, and return to
this day which has never been.

You Ask About Aging

Everything in nature erodes gracefully.
The tree leans and cracks. The mountain
rounds for decades in the wind. The banks
of the river bend to where the river wants to
go. But we, so aware of being here, fear the
slightest change. My elbow is sore. Your
heart is slowing down. And just yesterday,
an old friend flew away like a bird with a
broken wing. Still, for all I have learned,
for all I am learning, I don't want to go.
Though like the tree on the ridge that
has grown sideways toward the daily
twist of light, I see no greater destiny
or simplicity than to be stripped of all
pretense and want until all that's left is
a branch of being waiting for its wind.

The Inner Law

That the Universe comes through
your heart is like the sun passing
light through the eye of a needle.
It happens beyond all reasoning.

And though one feather will fall,
many together form a wing, the
way love, not kept to ourselves,
will carry us.

It is a deeper form of gravity,
that only the things that find
each other come alive.

Miraculum

Sometimes, when things
break, life begins. It still hurts.
But when the egg cracks, the
chick is born. When the dam
breaks, the fields finally grow.
And when the heart breaks, the
angels asleep for a hundred years
unfurl their wings and flutter
behind our eyes, letting us see
everything like Adam or Eve,
again. Then, miracle is not a
place we long for, but a blood
that brings us alive.

Responsibility

For a tree, it is to break ground
and bend with the wind.

For a fish, to find the current
and extract air from the deep.

For a bird, to glide and
return to its nest.

For a mind, to open
like a gate.

For a self, to let light move
through our humanness

by breaking, bending, finding,
extracting, gliding, returning,
and opening.

Four Quests

To loosen your mind is
to watch a crane without
making a sound.

To follow your heart is
to ride a dragon while
carrying a flower.

To accept one's fate is
to free the ox and make
a garden of the wheel.

To believe is to carve a
flute for the song not
yet written.

Just Now

a lost cardinal lands
on a winter branch
shaking off the snow
which drifts like
powdered sugar
on the squirrel
desperately trying
to climb the feeder
and, ever so quietly,
grace and effort meet.

The Gods Visit

They see everything from above,
how we dig in the fields and build
toward the sky, how we run from the
truth and never ask why. Our frailty
draws them to ride through the clouds
on horses made of wind. Then through
the mountains where they trot on waves
of snow. Then down through the streets
where we have forgotten them. Among
us, they remain invisible. We only see
the wind lift the trees, wishing we could
be as free. Seeing how heavy we are, they
toss spells in our way, which lure us from
our sadness for a while. When we persist,
they take on the shape of a problem or a
doubt. They stir up our being and hover
like a vow that waits for trouble to un-
lace the mind. Then, believing in us,
yet again, they mount and make their
way back to the sky, leaving us with
a sense that things could be better.

Book Three

THE TONE
IN THE CENTER
OF THE BELL

There is only one reality
and the only way to experience it
is to be real.
—PARKER J. PALMER

Make it plain.
Make it simple.
Make it sing.
—JOHN LEWIS

Shaped by the Oneness

Life can be harsh and beautiful by turns. Often, it seems unfair. Why can't the beautiful openings last longer? Over the years, I've learned that this movement from fullness to bareness and back is the inhalation and exhalation of the Universe. The rhythm is what keeps us alive. It keeps us growing. Once we open our heart, the thousand feelings come at us non-stop, the endless waves of a Mysterious Unity. How they wash over us and through us transforms us.

No matter how old or young, how willing or not, we are led to ask: What do we do with what we feel? By facing our struggles, we're asked to let all the feelings in and out so they can merge and bring us further into that depth which is the Unity of all Feeling.

At first, we see and comprehend Oneness. It's a breathtaking idea. I was excited and exhilarated as a young poet to have glimpses of Oneness, to understand that everything goes together, to understand that all life is somehow connected, even though we can't see how. Yet as I've grown and suffered and loved and lost, I've come to *feel* the Oneness of all Life.

So often we think we're alone while living our lives. In a deep way, we are, but we are never far from the life that connects us and the life that comes through us, if we can stay faithful to all that we feel.

The truth is that I would never have made it this far, if not for the note of Spirit filling me from within, shining out my eyes, making my hands reach for others, making my mind spread like a leaf. If not for that note of light, I'd be a hollow cave. This is the note of aliveness that makes us one family.

And the poems in this book, like the tone in the center of any bell, bear witness to the note of Spirit that rings through each of us as we are worn into exquisite shapes by the friction of the world, grounded by our suffering and lifted by love and wonder.

THE LOOSE DOGS
OF SANTIAGO

The blood of the children on the sidewalk
is like the blood of children on a sidewalk.

—PABLO NERUDA

The Way

When a horse runs, it leaps
and touches down by turns.

In just this way, our life is always
moving between joy and sorrow.

Trying to avoid this is its own
sorrow, like a mad bird trying
to escape the sky.

Rather, our call is to help each
other rise and help each
other land.

As if Anyone Knows

It takes a great disruption, of care or pain,
to drop below the veil. And what breaks
the trance—of all we've been taught about
why we're here, as if anyone knows—is,
of course, stunning and painful.

Most of us won't go below willingly.
Though it is the slowness of the
bottom that holds and renews.

I can see by your eyes that you held on
to the sheen of things too long like me.

But here we are, like clowns without
shoes with no tricks left. Now we can
break ground and wait for rain.

The Smoke of You

Old friend no longer a friend,
I'm tired of how you show up
in my dreams, how you call
and never say a word, how
you ask me to meet you
near the Wharf in San
Francisco, though you
never come.

I'm tired of remembering
the Miles Davis riff that
taught you so much, tired
of your dark rewrite of
everything, of the bear
of your anger swatting
at the world to protect
your wound.

I'm tired of cleaning up
the mess you leave in the
garden of my heart, tired
of sending my love for you
into space like a public
service announcement
by the Red Cross
after the war.

Sheltered-in-Place

I was walking our dog during the pandemic,
the neighborhood empty, the clouds heavy,
and, through my headphones, the music of
a man now gone, the love he couldn't hide
helping me keep my head above water. And
though it's hard to praise the vastness of the
sea when being pulled under, hard to believe
in the merit of light when lost in the dark,
hard to wait on love when painfully lonely—
these larger truths never stop being true.
Even as I voice this, someone is dying in
the hall of an overcrowded hospital, while
another is lifted from their own hell by the
grace of a kindness no one saw coming. As
if the spirit of the one dying arrives like pollen
in the heart of the one stuck in hell, giving them
just enough to begin again. If we could only give
the extra warmth we receive to someone who is
shivering. If we could shed the masks that
keep us from ourselves, there would be
enough to save the world.

Lightning in a Bottle

The being in us flies like a hawk.
It knows nothing of the ground.
But the human in us walks like
a horse and must climb over
everything. We grow by trying
to fly and suffer because we can't.

The Howl

In Chile, on the outskirts of
Santiago, hordes of loose dogs
howl as the sun goes down. Those
in the city who are hungry say they
howl for food. Those who are lonely
say they howl for love. And those
who are losing their sight say they
howl to remind the rest of us to
Stay Amazed! Every day at dusk, on
the ledge between light and dark,
their howl channels the suffering
of the world. The loose dogs of
Santiago voice the broken glass
of dreams. Their howl wakes us
to the moon in our tears.

Praxis

Whether pacing in a waiting
room or enduring a sudden throb
of pain, take a long breath and float
like a lily pad, spreading yourself
before the world while looking
for your tether to the bottom
of things.

Just float until your grip is
loosened. It will be alright.

After Mayo Clinic

She told me today that the surgery didn't
work and suddenly the earth opened up
and Hades started to pull her under. I'm
not ready for her to go but her soft kindness
is already casting light like dead stars that
illuminate the night. Like everyone before
me, I don't want her to die. Now, the others
that I've lost are peering back at me, as if
to say, "Don't you understand this yet?" I
turn from them wanting more than ever
to live, wanting her to live. The December
wind rushes through the leaves that are left.
Why do the brightest ones have to go first?

Stopped

—All music points
to something that
can't be broken.

I'm stopped by the old man
playing a dented sax on the
corner of University and 12th,
can feel the one tribe we are a
part of when someone in a hurry
turns around to help a blind
woman up the stairs of the
subway, guiding her to the
surface from the underworld
we've made. I squint and hope
someone will guide me.

Pain and Glow

We have shed many skins,
always working toward some
uncovered state: below opinion,
below expectation, even below
the exhilaration of a dream.
All to accept that shedding is
a way of life. Going out builds
up. Going in takes off. And we
go on. Despite the pain of taking
off, we want the glow of being to
last a bit longer. And we go on.
Now I see that this is how the
Universe renews itself: by build-
ing up and taking off. There is
no other way. Pain and Glow.
And we go on. Like a crab
inching from its shell. Like
a bird molting its feathers.
Like an enduring self leav-
ing everyone's judgments
on the side of the road.

Vigil

History is full of pearls
buried in mud. We all
hold vigil to find them.

Once in our hands,
a deeper play unfolds.
Some bite the pearl
to test its worth.

Some hide it again,
thinking that knowing
where it is will make
a difference.

But some, desperate
enough to love, swallow
the pearl that it might
flower in their wound.

Inside the King

We can stare out from our
castle all through the night.

Or scheme like a bishop
unsure of his worth.

Or rear our horse when
the world approaches.

But if we are to live, we
have to give up our throne,

step into the world,
and ask for help.

Daughter of Rta

(for Pam)

You have always looked into
the hearts of others in a way
that makes life our home.

When I think of the stories
you've held, I marvel at the
tapestry of your listening.

It led me to the word, ritual,
which you so love. It goes back
to the Sanskrit, *Rta*, which means
visible order. So, ritual makes the
order of the Universe visible.

Like the slow ritual of you
that has loved us so well.
Oh, Daughter of Rta, you
remind the pearl that it's
a pearl and the bird that
it can fly.

Facing the Question

Debris does not stay in one place
On a fast-running creek.

—Rumi

I hold on to my wounds because
I think caution will save me when,
like a stone tied to a pigeon's foot,
the weight of all that didn't work
will only keep me from building
my nest.

Yet, I cannot pretend I was not cut
or left for dead. I must understand
why I let those I loved hurt me. What
treasure did I think they had that was
waiting inside, for me to grow?

As He Lay There

When my father was close
to death, we were stripped
of our history. I sat by his bed,
holding the ancient, twig-like
hand of a ninety-three-year-old
who, though absent for years,
was mythic to me.

As he lay there, under the weight
of a stroke, life undressed the myth
I put on him and he was just a frail
old man who had introduced me
to the sea, who had loved wood
into marvelous shapes, who sur-
rounded himself with books
though he was a slow reader.

After a lifetime of holding back,
he wanted to speak, though he
couldn't. And I understood
him completely.

On the Move

A sudden breeze under the moon
brings a whisper of other life and
then, a fox trotting in the open, as
if to say, there are many scenes
happening at once under this
moon.

The breeze lifts and with it the
scent of troubled souls on the
move, giving what they have
to those who stay behind.

The fox wouldn't say
who they are or what they give,
just beckoned me to follow.

Walkabout

So many of us walk about in a prison
of thought given to us by others. And
looking for love, we suffer. Until one
day, unable to keep it together, we are
broken of all thought and everything
is new and old at once. Everything is
unlived before we live it. Now, there
are tears for the nearest bit of life:
the worm lost on the sidewalk, the
red scarf pinned by wind to a wire
fence, the soft note escaping
your heart.

Inside the Pandemic

Now that we can't touch, I am awash
with all the ways that touch sustains us:
like an electricity from one heart to another
or the rush of ancient water down a falls into
the basin of a village. I'm thinking of how you
wiped my brow in the hospital, and the time
you stroked a fallen bird, its beak aquiver,
and the time your mother held your face,
saying, "I saw how loving you are the day
you were born." Or the moment I caught
a stranger in the parking lot as her groceries
splattered, her cart wobbling away. Earlier,
it was Grandma hoisting me to my feet in
her Brooklyn alley and the hands of my
father guiding mine as he taught me to
use a chisel. Now I'm seeing Whitman
as a medic in the Civil War wrapping a
bandage around a corporal's chest. And
now I close my eyes to send my touch,
like a Shaman across the dreamscape,
hoping it will reach you.

Atlas Tires

At last, I quiet myself until
I sink below the weight and
agitation, below the yak of
who's done what to whom. I
even let go my need to carry
everything. I sink without a
care until the silence swallows
me. Let the world fall into itself.
What is is enough. Below, I float
and sway like a broken shell in
a net of kelp. Down here, I
am washed of all the grit.

A Little Slower
Than I Imagined

A heel comes down hard in mud. It
freezes this way in winter. In spring,
it rains until the footprint is gone,
though the memory of the heel coming
down never goes away. We live like this.

Then, a small bird drops a feather which
lands before you and you pick it up as
an omen that you must lighten your way.
You put the feather on your dashboard
and every time you see it, you turn the
music up. We live like this, too.

Knowing What We Know

Oh! I have loved you from the beginning!
I just didn't know it! We are only strangers
till we wake. "But how do I know this is real?"
you ask. When you put your hand in
water, do you have to ask if it's wet?

Beyond the Reef

As a boy, the wind through large willows
let me see truth without its features. Later,
in the Rockies, the vastness let me glimpse
eons before we were here. And being ill,
near death, was a vastness all its own that
stunned me back to life. Since waking a
second time, the face of every friend has
been a lake in which I rest when bruised.
Now solitude is a lighthouse, the beam
within scanning the depths for tender
souls, calling them closer, pointing
out the rocks that lay between us.

In August

The light bobs on the
small leaves, so quietly,
so thoroughly, that I can
feel its ancestor bow
along a bend in the Yangtze
River a thousand years ago.

I sense my counterpart
imagining me a thousand
years in the future.

Like two souls looking
through a window they
mistake for a mirror, we
settle back into ourselves.

The chord we strike
fills each of us with a sense
of Eternity we can't forget.

The Earth grudgingly turns
away from the sun and the
leaves now in shade are
just leaves in shade.

But we have each seen
all the way through.

Each of us left with an
urge to be more loving.

A Pearl of Wind

Tell me a story, any story. Tell me
what happened or what didn't happen
or what you hope will happen. I need
signs of life to lift my head. I need some
pearl of wind to open my wing. So sing
me a song. For yourself, but let me listen.
I don't care if you're trained or shy or
can't hum a tune. Just sing anything.
It will stir my heart. We can do this
for each other, can't we? It's not like me
to ask so plainly. But I left my curiosity
in the back of the car when picking up
the groceries and now I'm waiting for
the nearest cloud to burst with rain, to
wash away the noise. As soon as the
wonder returns, I will sing for you.

A Panoply

Feelings stir within and rise
like notes skipping off the piano,
floating through the hours, land-
ing in the bread aisle at the grocery
store, and on the handle of the gas
pump, and on the tree you leaned
against when out of breath. And
though we must face what comes
from within, we carry untold stories
from lives we barely know. So when
we meet without a word while wait-
ing in line at Starbucks, trust that
we are completing each other, no
matter our fear of being alone.
Even now, you are picking up
a grain of story from me, like
a smudge of pollen or ash.

This Way and That

Like you or me, he was always on
the move, this time on a train. Like
you or me, he loved to sit by the window,
humming as the world sped by. The sun
on the mountains struck a chord. He felt
an ache for those he'd left and those he'd
lost. He could almost see their faces in
the hills. Like you or me, feeling what
had come to pass made him sink into
the hollow of his chest. So when the train
stopped at a small station built before the
war, he got out to stretch his legs. It was
then that something in the wind made him
cross the tracks. And the sway of old trees
made him forget himself. As in a dream,
the thing in him that had no name would
wander that field forever, while the thing
in him refusing to be found would get
back on the train, looking from window
to window, not sure for what.

Irrepressible Star

As the Earth bows slowly toward
the sun, someone with a fever is
dreaming that she's drowning while
someone else is giving birth to a child
who will one day save a stranger from
taking his life by stopping in the rain
to touch his elbow, asking, "Are you
alright?" So despite the thousands
of mirrors that keep us from each
other, the smallest gesture stirs us
in time for the sun to flood us
with this thing we call morning.

What Gate Is This?

Once through this gateway, you wander
all heaven and earth in a single stride.

—WUMEN

Is it the gate I fell through
while having a rib removed?

Or the gate I collapsed through
When my father died?

Or the gate I leapt through
when realizing I couldn't live
without you?

Or the one I shimmied through
when finally putting down
all that doesn't matter?

The heart is a gate that opens
and shuts a thousand times—
our version of wings.

Undone

How can I carry this?
When your hands are in the
water, you can't carry water.

How can I stop this?
The wind strips the tree
of all its leaves.

How can I believe?
Light through a crack
fills the entire cave.

But how do I know?
Before mirrors, we closed
our eyes and simply listened.

Inside the Mirror

For years, when things got tough,
he'd dream of being a cloud, having
no idea that the cloud, tired of being
blown about, dreamt of being a person
or an animal wandering the earth. And
wanting to quiet his rush of words, he
had no idea that Spirit was looking
for clear souls to rush through, the
way wind will stir the song out of trees.
He kept trying to find himself in other
life, never knowing that other life was
rushing to enter him, the way water
is destined to fill a hole.

Being There

Everyone in the house
is hurting. And I feel
powerless. Oh, I can
bandage this and make
tea and listen.

Yet all I can do is feel
their pain. Like trees
falling in a lake, I can
only let them rest in me.

Sometimes, we're given
more than we can carry,
which makes us return
to carry more. And the
things we can't carry,
we care for and watch.

Eventual Fall

For all my talk, let me
listen like the sun.

For all my resistance, let
me serve like the surf.

For all my hesitation, let
me be as steadfast as a cliff.

Let my deepest fear
be as armless as a stone,

so I can sink into the
assurance of all that is.

I will meet you in the
bareness that waits.

Slow Growing

A properly pruned Japanese
Maple is one that a bird can
fly through because the spaces
are as important as the leaves.
And a properly pruned mind
is decluttered so that what we
don't know can come through.

A Teacher's Confession

Wherever I go, I find the story
of how we carry what can't be
carried until it breaks in our
hands and there is nothing
left but to give everything
away.

And I listen like a prism,
blessed to have the honey
of others sweeten the way.

People thank me, but it is I
who am brought alive like a
vacant jewel—only a gem
when the light of others
passes through me.

The Tone
in the Center
of the Bell

No matter where you look—
near, far, up, down, out or in—
there is a bareness of being that
lives in the center of every ounce
of life, the way air waits inside
every bubble as it rises from
the deep. The way a small
pocket of worth waits inside
every attempt to love. The way
wonder waits in the center
of our heart for something to
wake it. The tone keeps ringing
in the center of the bell, long after
our ears stop hearing it. Whether
we know this or not, this is how
life moves through the living,
how light makes a branch grow
toward it. How a stream draws
a horse to drink from it.
How you draw me to ask
what it is to be you.

The Metrics
of Seeing

*If you understand, then you can put down
your shield and spear on the hundred grasses.*

— Hsiang Lin

The Great Waters

In the beginning, I thought I was
going somewhere. I thought we all
were. But falling in while trying to cross,
I finally understood, the journey is to follow
the river. All the rivers, especially the ones
no one can see. The soul is a fish whose
home is in those rivers. So I can take you
across, if you want. But the secret is to go
everywhere by going nowhere. And I will
be here when you fall in. Which is not
a failure but an awakening.

Try As We Do

As a truck runs a light, side-
swiping a van, a hummingbird,
three blocks away, hovers over a
small red feeder, working for a sip
of nectar, lifting to swallow, bow-
ing to sip, like a half-formed angel,
unable to voice what it has learned
about life on Earth. The drivers
crawl from the wreck, lucky to
be alive. Try as we do, the things
that matter are not ours to give.
They can only be received, from
a grace that covers everything like
a cloud weighed down with honey.

Secret of the Night

You called the hotel to say that
Zuzu had killed a possum.

It was lying near the birdfeeder
with its tongue sticking out.

You were so upset
and I was so far away.

You said, "I'll have to bury it."
I said, "Use the snow shovel
and put it in the woods,"
thinking, *Let it stay in the
labyrinth of nature.*

In the morning, it was gone.
You were relieved but compelled
to find out more.

You texted me on the plane:
*It is an unconscious reflex that
lets them enter that state when
they are threatened.*

They seem to go away
until what is hunting them
leaves them alone.

If we could only learn how.
You could have gone there
as a child when your father

came home drunk and full
of rage.

And I could have gone there
when my mother slapped my
face extra hard because I asked
why she was mean.

I'm 35,000 feet up, wanting
the possum to teach us, so we
who have been threatened might
meet there like a crowd of stars
out of reach of all harm.

Wild Rock Dove

In WWII, the French, hoping
to escape Nazi occupation, sent
homing pigeons with pleas for help.
They would kiss their gray wings and
let them fly into the night. Once in
a while, a pigeon would land in the
window of a stranger who would be
startled by something prophetic falling
from the sky. Often, the plea would be
read as a revelation dropped by an angel
to make them face the truth of their life.
And I confess, I have tied my small plea
in code when desperate and alone and
let it fly into the night, praying it will
reach someone filled with love
who by some miracle might
find me after the war.

Beneath the Wind

We are the only creatures who
argue over how to find the light.

The branches in the forest bend
and stretch freely for the sun.

And birds, surprised by wind,
simply spread their wings.

But we need a dozen reasons,
just to begin. When, as with

love, there are no pros and
cons in being a flame.

Behind Our Face

We start out innocent enough.
We want to be liked and well thought
of. So we wear that want like a mask
we show everyone. It fits so well that in
time we forget it's a mask. Then, one day
we have an itch below our good eye and,
try as we do, we can't reach it. Now, there's
a lining between us and the world. And
everything, from the watered flowers
to the pain of our lover, seems distant,
almost gray. And not able to touch what
is near makes us sad in a way we can't
seem to shake. Then, one day in the rain,
we stop with our head in our hands, feeling
desperate for life which is so close but so far.
And crying in the middle of the street, our
face falls off and shatters on the sidewalk.
Just then, someone we have dismissed or
overlooked happens by. She stops to pick
up the jewels that were trapped behind
our face. She gives them to us saying,
"You are so blessed" though we feel
anything but blessed. And the sun
pushes through the dark clouds as
we eat the jewels that were ours
from the beginning.

Life Tracks

My mother taught me
how to build a wall.
My father showed me
how to climb it.

They never said so
but they loved the wall
and called it home.

In time, I grew like
a chick in its shell.

Inevitably, I cracked
the wall to live my life.

They never forgave me.

Climbing

I was in Vancouver, sitting
in the brilliant sun on a bench
along English Bay, sensing the
deeper order under everything,
when I suddenly felt you sitting
on a similar bench somewhere
in the world.

We are saved by these compelling
spaces. Like the alcove in Florence
I chanced upon, two feet wide, in
which an angel's head had broken
off and she lay staring up from
the cobblestone.

Bare spaces like the open palm of
my friend's day-old son. I couldn't
move from the glass as this insect
of a being flexed his tiny hand,
already looking to grip before
he could see.

They say ice climbers scale frozen
waterfalls while the water keeps
rushing below the ice.

The way we climb the days, the
invisible Source flowing below
everything that has hardened
within us and between us.

Long Way Down
the Mountain

The squinty one calibrates how
far he's gone and what markers will
make it easy to return, while the soft
one waits for the wind to tell him what
needs to be tended. This war between
carrying and tending never ends. And
I have wasted life after life seeking what
to haul and how to sell it. When what I
really need is to know how things in life
fit. All for the chance to offload some
gold, so I can help you up and
take you home.

Remembering

Does a tree remember last year's
storm? Does a doe recall cutting
itself on that broken fence? Are
we the only ones who build
trenches in the past?

Should we use memory more
like an oar, stroking it in our
consciousness to make our
way forward?

Still, I remember where we broke
and how we mended, can feel the
rush of heart when we first met
and the collapse inside when
my father died.

How to go back and not drown?
How to cleanse where we've
been, like a doe washing its
cut in a mountain stream?

The Metrics of Seeing

It felt strange to teach again
after my surgery, as if I'd made it
through some dark tunnel, and there
were young minds at the end, as if
they'd been waiting there all along.

And not very far into our first
session, a bright thin one—teetering
on the edge of all he'd taken in and
organized in his short unexpected life—
blurted out, "Alright, so you almost
bought it. What's the point?"

He was poised, ready
to jot down my wisdom.

I said, "I don't know."

He dropped his pen,
exasperated.

I went to him,
"I'm sorry.
I do know."

He picked up his pen.
I said, "In here,"
I touched his chest,
"the heart knows all."

"In here," I touched my own,
"the heart has its eyes."

He was scribbling.
I put down his pen.

"Up here," I tapped his head,
"the mind never rests, trying
to earn what the soul assumes."

He stared at me.

I patted him on the shoulder,
"You see," I touched my heart,
"I do know," then tapped my head,
"but I don't."

The Physics
of Commotion

When a lake is clear, it reflects
the whole sky. When disturbed,
it mimics the point of disturbance.

Yet even when disturbed, we get
the chance to find the sacred
wherever we land.

And when things break down,
we must discern what needs to be
repaired, what needs to be reimagined,
and what needs to stay dismantled.

Never forget that difficulty
concentrates growth, the way
night makes stars visible.

Out of View

Letting go of all I've been taught
is like spilling a bag of marbles
on a hill and watching them
bounce out of view.

Though each was there
to remind me of something
profound, without them I am free
to name everything in the world
all over again.

The Agreement

Like someone who falls
from a height into the water,
I'm past the fall and living
in the depth I fell into.

Now I must plant two seeds,
for I know one will be washed
away in the storm.

Now I must give more than
take, so care can split the
mud of our ways.

Now I must accept death,
in order to feel the shimmer
each time we wake.

The Effortless Work

In my twenties and thirties,
I kept reacting to the duality of life
until I was thrown below it.

Now, in between my troubles,
I sense the things that boil in the pot
of human traffic and feel compelled
to translate what I see in the eyes of
those wanting to live and in the
slouch of those wanting to die.

To hear each other requires work
and no work at all. The way a shore
doesn't work to hear the sea, though
the smallest gull must wing its way
from surf to surf.

The November Wind

is freeing the trees of the leaves
that hang on. How can I be freed
of my stubbornness?

When ripped of what we want,
we think the world so cruel. In time,
though never soon enough, we start
to glisten and rise again. We never
seem to learn that this is the rhythm.

Now the tennis ball I throw my dog
is lost in the swell of leaves. I know
it's there. I'll find it come spring,
buried under all we can't hold
or do without.

Feeling Thorough

Sometimes, when the moon is full,
a horse will gallop through the forest
and cross the stream, just to feel its
heart pound in the open. Or a man
will get up and chop wood until there
is nothing left to split. Often, we must
give our all in order to feel the calm
of centuries waiting in the stillness.
It's what marathoners feel the instant
they stop, hands on their knees, what
dancers feel the moment the dance
ends and their arms drop, what you
and I feel the moment we are honest
with each other. I've come to see that
love is the horse and truth is the axe.

Immeasurable

Sometimes, when winded
by a loss I didn't see coming,
I lean on the edge of the hive,
unsure how to continue. That
is when, having dropped all my
plans, I stare into the vastness
in which we rise and fall. And
like a broken watch sinking in
the sea, I feel held by the deep
though my purpose is gone.

Turning to You
(for Robert)

A still heart like a still leaf will
let light through in a way that
makes the woodpecker in our
mind stop long enough for the
throb in our head to ease.

We can't stay there because we
live in the world. But we can re-
turn. And on days I can't stop
worrying or imagining the worst,
I long to sit with you in the sun
because you are such a leaf.

Humbly

Under all trouble,
like a broom sweeping
broken glass, is "I'm
sorry" and "I love you"
waiting like the edge
of a waterfall.

The Voyage

So many notes to arrive
at the one that touches
silence.

So many words to arrive
at the opening that reveals
what remains wordless.

So many loves to arrive
at the isness of being
that some call God.

Cascade

As soon as we can walk, we are
taught to run. In time, we think
we have to catch something out
of reach, when, if we let go, time
carries us the way a river carries a
boat with no oars. If we find our
place on the bottom, the noise stops
and time holds us in its soft cascade.
So jump into the current of time.
Sure, we will get wet. But that's the
point. Important papers will dry and
seem less important. And the secret
maps, once torn and lost, will free us
from ourselves. I once saw an old
woman leave her belongings on
the shore and wade in naked. I
feared she might be taking her
life. But she was finally giving
herself over to joy.

Genetic Drift

There is something beautiful
about being precise. How dolphins
use sponges to protect their beaks
while digging for food and crows
in Japan drop nuts in front
of cars to crack them open.

Our ancestors whittled tools
out of bone and stitched blankets
from fur. And though we have
every convenience, we still make
spoons out of what we've been
through to sip from what can last.

A healer I know uses an ancient
stone to rub a cramp from your
calf. This is why we read, to rub
the cramp from our mind.

If we love something enough,
it becomes a wheel or a wing.
In time, we become small levers
by which others move what
is forever in the way.

Laws of Motion

I think of you, now gone, and
drop my care like a pebble into
the lake of time.

I can name it as a longing for
you which it is, but more, it is
that–which–never–dies holding
us together beneath all our
suffering.

The maples on the far hill bend
because of a wind we can't see,
the way my heart bows toward
everything, living or not.

There is no light without shadow,
no love without grief, no ripple
without the drop of the stone.

To Coalesce

When I feel what I hold
and listen with my heart,
I drink from what we
have in common.

Then, our pain can't be
separated from our wonder,
any more than you can find
a vein of gold without lifting
the stone that carries it.

A Small Trio

When insight comes,
it reveals the spaces
in the mind, the way
light in the morning
unfurls the tops
of trees.

When acceptance
comes, it tears the
massive web we
didn't know we
were weaving.

Then grace appears,
to make us bow like
a peony back toward
the ground it came
from,

surprised it lived
long enough
to blossom.

Where the Bow
Holds the Arrow

It's the frame that calls us into the
painting and the window that pulls us
into the world. And no matter how a
train grumbles to be free, it is betrothed
to its tracks. As I, despite my want to
fly, am destined for the ground.

Under the Quest

Can you drink from the Lake of Being
you came from before you were named?

For peace lives there.

I don't mean for you to undo your life
or to leave the world but to put down

all that has proven false so you can taste
from what is lasting which is always near.

And here's the mountain which when
crossed is worth the journey—
can you be such a lake to others?

Giving Back

In this long and quiet day,
I chance to glimpse the Eternal
as it seeps through the smallest
detail: lip of cup, dip of wind,
stretch of light across the table
as steam rises from my tea.

Now our dog leaps from the
deck into the snow, so happy
to be in a body off the ground.
I feel the same when lifted
by these moments.

I carry these small wonders
like drops of Mystery to leave
wherever I notice suffering,
so that, like water softening
paper, love might soften pain.

Art Lesson

The mind moves like a pencil.
The heart moves like a brush.

While the mind can draw
exquisite prints, the heart
with its deep bright colors
will ignore the lines.

If you only follow your mind,
you will never go outside the lines.

If you only follow your heart,
what you touch will never
resemble anything.

We must be
a student of both.

For the mind can build
itself a home, but only
the heart can live in it.

For All

By now, I should know, there
is no end to this undoing. I just
keep being opened to some
indestructible tenderness
that keeps life going.

Now, I only want to watch
the sun soften the trees, to
watch the braille of waves
defy my need to understand
them.

Only want to watch you smile
in the dark of a theater where
we take off our differences
long enough to admit
we are each other.

Anyway

While the sleeping
rose forgives the sun
that wakes it, and the
startled fish thanks the
falls for bringing it to
the sea, it's harder for
the feeling heart to
forgive the pain
that opens it.

The Integrity
of Color

We drive by the maple
all year long but only in
October are we stunned
enough to stop as it turns
orange. If I could only be
this thorough, to accept
the very air so completely
that I would glow without
going anywhere. This is
the magnetism of the soul
coming through the body
that contains it. And the
color entering the leaves
shows us what might
happen if we could
empty all intent. But
far from this, we watch,
as the tree sheds its
brilliance, a filament
of all we long to be.

How We Arrive

It doesn't matter how we arrive,
just that we do. Tolstoy wrote thirteen
drafts of the first chapter of *War and
Peace*. He kept circling what matters
like a hawk sensing something
stirring underground.

And having gathered 42 poets
at Orchid Pavilion, Wang Xizhi
floated cups of wine downstream
and those who lifted the cups had to
compose a poem or drink the wine.

At the end of this day in 353 AD,
37 poems had been retrieved and
Wang wrote his *Preface to the Poems
Composed at Orchid Pavilion* right
there with his feet in the stream.

Years later, Emperor Taizong, who
achieved greatness by not responding
to criticism or praise, admired Wang's
calligraphy so much that he had the
original *Preface* buried with him.

Though we may never see it coming,
we can be cracked open by the storm
or become wise like the axle of an
old wagon growing tarnished
season by season.

It is said that Wang learned how
to turn his wrist while stroking his
brush by watching geese move their
necks between the sky and their
reflection in the water.

A Shift of Mind

After all these years,
I immerse now more than extract
and quiver more than conclude.

Somewhere along the way,
I stopped looking and started
entering, putting my whole
self in without reservation.
This has made the difference.

Often, when drawn under,
we fear we are sinking, when
we are being pulled into a depth
that will change everything.

It happens when I fear the intensity
of you being you, only to be softened
by a synapse of care that holds
us all. Then I no longer resist,
letting you and your pain
into my heart.

And all the while, the eddy
of life-force slows till we are
dropped below illusion.

This Keeps Us Sane

You drink the water before I ladle
it into these cups that we call poems.

You hear the song that is stirring
before it makes a sound.

You see the question in my
wonder, as I tuck before I fly.

I would be lost without you, like
one leg, one thought, one wheel.

THE INSIDE OF JADE

I hope you will go out and let stories happen to you, and that you will work them, and water them with your blood and tears and laughter till they bloom, till you yourself burst into bloom.

—CLARISSA PINKOLA ESTÉS

Summer Is Leaving

The wind is up—not a gust but no
longer a breeze. The clouds skirt by,
as if blown about by a hidden god,
not to lift us but to point to that
scent of nothing we all need to
begin again. At this time of year—
a sudden light, a sudden shade. In
these moments, we can try on joy
and sorrow, side by side. Whole lives
made visible, just for a second. As if
knowing this makes the choices
any easier.

Pierced

I first saw the part of Susan
I have known forever when
sitting near a statue of Moses
in Washington Park. I sat
under his staff for hours.

And during a thunderstorm,
Paul and I jumped in Hunt
Lake to swim in the rain. We
were thoroughly cleansed.

And when George and I flew
across the country to stand on
Bald Mountain, we felt forty
years of wind comb the land
off the Pacific. It lifted us like
crazy birds.

Before all this, I woke from
surgery with Robert holding
a washcloth to my fevered
head. And I wept.

These brief rescues
punctured my story and let
me know that Eternity is
in the Center of Now.

In the Alley

When young, the light
on the broken bit of glass
in the alley made it seem a gem.

It took years but now I know—
the broken bit of glass
is a gem.

From a distance, so much
seems more or less. But in time
love and suffering reveal
things as they are.

When young, I thought that
Heaven was over the hill.

Only to find that Heaven
is what holds us when putting
anything broken in the light.

After the War

How can I be a bridge
to help you cross what
you need to cross?

This is finally all I aspire to.
To reach across the divide
because I have been so divided.

To pick up what is broken
because I have done the breaking.

To ask for guidance because I
too have been so stubborn.

Seeing Things Through

If we only use the self as
a refuge from the outer
world, it remains a cave.

But keep going inward and
the self opens to a canyon
whose river of voices will
carry us while reflecting
the heavens.

Yet no one can stay that
far in and live.

We are meant to tend the
self as a passageway, trying
not to fear the things that
nest in us to avoid the
storm, but to give them
shelter.

Ancestral

Our yellow lab follows me
and looks at me intently,
as if I have answers to
questions she doesn't
know how to ask.

All I can do is look back
and lean my head into hers.

We snort each other and
she puts her paw on my
elbow as I rub her silky
ear. In the anonymous
afternoon, we echo our
ancestors curling by some
fire on the ancient plain.

Gateways

I love the small questions
that work like hinges in the
world, that creak open the
edge of Mystery. Like what
makes cows stop grazing to
watch the sun go down? Or
how is the center of every
storm so calm? Or how
does light find every crack?

I love the small gestures
that work like oars in the
sea of trouble. Like when
you stopped the car to move
a turtle out of the road. Or
when an old friend went to
seven stores to get the one
kind of juice I could keep
down while on chemo.

I love to glimpse the unsee-
able truth that holds every-
thing together. Like the
patch of light from the sun
that bounces off Orion's belt
to pause a hundred seekers
when the light spills
on their face.

Or when the thing that
stirred this poem reaches
through me to you the
moment these words
pull aside the veil.

In Don's Kitchen

—It's the moments that glow
that convince me we are truly here.

George and I were watching the snow
swirl when Don called out, "Hey! Look
what I found!" He appeared with an old
accordion on his chest. He held it like
an old friend who'd been asleep and
said, "I bought this forty years ago for
ten dollars." It was chipped and faded.
He tried to play but the strap was broken
and it was too heavy to keep going. Some-
thing made me step behind him to hold
the strap so he could pump the years away.
And he unfolded like an orchid that had
bloomed in another time. It somehow
makes sense that being held will open
our song.

What Love Remains

The sudden wind makes the tree
wake up and think it's going somewhere
but all that's happened is that the birds
have been forced to fly for a while and
some leaves have been lost because
they couldn't hang on.

This is how you come to me, father,
after years of being gone. And I still
fly after you.

And this is how you tease me, mother,
though there was never anything to
hold onto between us.

And this is how I send what love
remains, my brother. For though
you're here, you're out of reach.

I rustle with the past and go
nowhere, like a great tree
shaken of its affections.

I Can Watch

I can watch bits of light
rim the edges of morning—
as it did just now—and not need
to name it God or entropy.

Isn't it enough to bow to this
invisible energy jetting from the sun,
only to be seen on the lip of my plate?

Isn't it more instructive to let it
live beyond the confines of what-
ever name we might give it?

This is the conversation I was
born into below our attempts
at speech.

And yet, these moments have
led me into a river of words.

At times, it seems more holy
not to name anything. More
liberating to let it quietly
move through us.

Is It Possible?

That when moved to speak from
our heart, we are lifting a cup
from the One Water that all
souls drink from?

That every poem ever written is
part of one continuous voice, the
way every fire no matter how lit
reveals the same luminous flame?

That when I hold you, we are
in the swell of everyone who has
ever been held in the long silken
unfolding of time?

Is it possible that when I dare to
open my mind beyond all I've been
taught, I am awakened by that
which never dies?

Under the Snow

Across the years, my drift into
understanding has been like a
hawk descending in glide, one
spiral after another, until I have
landed where flight is no longer
necessary.

And my breakdown into peace
has been like a cliff standing up
to the sea, until after all my suffer-
ings, I only long to join, until with
each crumble, I utter, "Take me."

Now, my ability to give is ever
increased by my acceptance of
surrender, like a dandelion
finally giving way to the
slightest gust of wind.

Aquiver

Everything in life constricts and
dilates: the knots in our mind, the
cramps in our heart. When things
tighten, we twist in the torque of
the Universe. When things unwind,
the loosening of life is peace. Like
today, the sun is strong, the breeze
is slight, and the cherry blossoms
sway almost imperceptibly. Though
it can't last, we rise in a bubble of
being without going anywhere,
as the edge of the blossom
quivers, an inch of Heaven.

For George

What I love about you most
is how you become what you
care for. You are eager to begin,
but in no hurry to leave. And so,
when you offered to build a bookcase
in which my tall wooden Ganesh can
look over me as I dive into the ancient
swirl of secrets that are only secret
because we refuse to become what
we care for—it made me love you more.
It took many seasons and you shared
every step, from the soft pencil design
to taking off my closet doors to make
sure the dream would fit. Then, the
list of materials and the choice of a
proper light, so that every time I'd
turn, I could see Ganesh bow to the
unbendable truth that what's in the
way is the way. For months, we dis-
cussed the grain of wood, the number
of shelves, the placing of Ganesh like
truth at eye level, the curve of molding
that would crown the ancient god who
I have come to trust as much as I trust
you. The walnut now holds my books
hauled up from the deep. And while
I work hard to see what waits beneath
the masks we cling to, the precision of
your care holds everything in place.

There Is
This Choice

After the rain, the trees sway
like old rabbis lost in prayer,
as if their sway brings another
day, as if swaying is the key to
survival, as if bending is how
we make it through the storm.

Those in pain sway like trees,
only to bow and sigh when
the pain goes.

It is the sway that lets us slip
through trouble, the bow
that lets us settle into peace.

From space, it must seem like
everything on Earth is swaying
or bowing to some unnamable
force.

Keep Trying

Take off your situation
and you are closer.

Take off the story you've
been told about yourself
and you are closer still.

Take off your dream of
compliance or rebellion
and you're almost there.

Take off your name and
put your face in the stream
of all that wants to fill you.

Jump Rope

As rivers make things
sprout from the earth,
Spirit makes us reach
for each other.

And wind clears a path
for birds to glide between
long branches, the way
grace eases us through the
stumble of days.

When the heart opens,
nothing matters but the
sudden lift from pain or
fear.

Like a child who keeps
jumping to feel that instant
of weightlessness, we keep
loving.

For Those Who Still Meet Life with Song

Perhaps all beauty is in the dab
of taste on the tongue. Perhaps we
can't see everything until we enter
the smallest thing.

Perhaps the pianist, head down, eyes
closed, plays the same rumble of notes,
over and over, until he falls into the
canyon of emptiness from which
all music comes.

Perhaps, when split by a moment of
love that won't let me stay the same,
I am falling into the one truth that
every soul is led to when that ache
won't go away.

On certain days, it's clear that music
was conceived so the heart can glide
for a time without its burden.

Under the Waves

While everything outside is
wearing us down, everything
inside is wearing us free.

All that's left is to break
surface like a whale.

So I dive my way through
time, each day the parting
of a sea.

Until truth spreads like
moonlight, turning all
our thoughts blue.

The Real Gold

I dreamt that whatever each
of you needed, I was able to
fill with a piece of my heart
and far from being diminished,
my heart kept growing each time
I gave. Soon, I realized that each
of you were filling me with halos
of care. Then, I woke and saw that
this is how living things heal, by
this anonymous giving that lets
the cut mend with barely a scar.
This is how we start again when
everything has burned. Now I
run quietly through the days,
touching everything.

How We Rehearse

We are new and old at once,
arriving where we begin, learning,
over and over, that we were whole
with our first breath.

In this way, the heart rehearses
its opening and closing, the way
a bird migrates over the same
stretch of earth, year after year.

Yet the mind keeps chewing
on its themes, the way an old
fish nibbles in the crevice of
its reef.

We start out certain there is
a secret, only to discover that
silence is our home.

Nesting

Part of the mind is
always full of thoughts,
the way a nest is full
of twigs.

Because we sleep and
wake there, we forget
that the bird itself
with its ability to
leave the nest is
the saving grace
of the mind.

What No One Owns

Once the leaves are brilliant, they
tear away and float across the path,
stopping us no matter where
we're going.

This is the fate of brilliant ideas.
They leave the mind and float
between us, making sure we
remember that all that is
brilliant is just passing
through.

So, make your lists of what
you have and what you want.

If blessed, the game of want
and dream is all used up like
stories in the paper crumpled
to start a fire.

At Sea with Time

Energy is time compressed
as when a bow is drawn
before the arrow flies.

Agitation is time held onto
as when a cowboy tries
to tame a horse.

And peace comes when
entering time as when a fish
slips into the strongest
current.

We move through these
states constantly the way
water begins in a cloud,
condenses into rain, then
flows around everything,
only to be heated into
steam.

And so, the wheel of
wonder, worry, joy.

Casting a Wide Net

When struggling to stay afloat, I had
a dream of learning how to breathe
underwater. That was twenty years ago.

Now, I walk through the days but live
in the deep.

Now, I swim with others to the bottom
and retrieve what we see as our teachers.

Sometimes, to dream is to learn how
to live like a knot unraveling.

No Name for This

Under all that happens, we are
forced to admit what's true, the
way a flower opens in rain.

Then the irreducible center
shows itself with no purpose
other than its own beauty.

And we wonder, why all the
fuss to be other than we are.

Far enough in and beauty
and truth shed their names.

This was how I found them
in the waters between us so
many years ago.

It is a sea I return to when
I put things down and listen.

Coming Up for Air

The times are hard and unexpected.
They always are. But the river of being
that carries us is always life-giving,
if we can reach it.

This, as ever, requires diving where
we are, not running from what is.
We must be brave and must beware,
mostly of ourselves.

For the mind is like a spider. It will
weave many webs. But the heart is like
an arrow of light. It will pierce a hole
in the dark that life will fill.

Along the way, we stumble in the dark.
Our fierce and tender honesty, the lamp
we swing between us.

Still Point

As I drift down the river,
slouched in the open boat
that is my life, I dip my hand
below the surface and everything
slows. It has always been this way.

A slight breeze lifts my face and
I forget where I'm going and where
I've been. Just then, the one cloud
moves to the east and the sun
fills my life.

The warmth closes my eyes
and I remember each of you.

And all we did and all we couldn't
manage peel away like petals which
had to open in order to know
this fragrance.

Able to Touch

If still enough and tender enough,
we are able to touch the center of
the Universe, the way a sage, three
days from his death, touches the
center of his reflection in a lake,
feeling that softness ripple into
everything.

Offering in Blue

May you meet each day with
your head to the sky and your
feet on the ground. May you
repair the world by offering
your gift to others.

May you find the courage to
carry what needs to be carried
and the surrender to let
yourself be held until
you blossom.

Keep listening for the poem
being written in your heart.
It will speak truth to you
the way wind parts the sea.

Finding It

How will you ever find peace
unless you yield to love?

—Rabia

If you put down what you carry
in case of emergency, you will make
space for what can really help. For
clutching onto failure or success
will only distract you.

And hiding in your fear will
only make you a dark house
that no one can enter.

So unlatch the cage you have
double-locked and watch the
dark things fly.

There is a nameless drop of
honey inside every dream and
scheme. Finding it is not a reward
and missing it is not a punishment.
Its quiet appearance is, at last, a
small harmonic opening in
response to presence.

In Those Moments

Sometimes, after she falls and before
she gets up, she takes a deep breath.
And in those moments, she stares
briefly into the Center of Things.
It calms her. For in those moments,
she drinks from something older than
her life. Other times, the same thing
happens when reading a passage from
a book that opens her heart. Or when
hearing that lift in a song that makes
her think of looking at the stars as
a little girl. She never knows how to
speak of these openings. It's as if
the still point of her life rests on
the bottom of all trouble like a
weighted pearl. And an invisible
string ties it to her heart. And
every once in a while, the pearl
of life tugs at her heart, forcing
her to fall and remember that
there is nowhere to go.

View at Seventy

I'm standing on a bridge
near the top of a mountain,
looking back at the winding
path that took years to climb.
And there, below, the chasm
I thought I'd never cross, much
more beautiful on this side of
the rise. And in the vastness
that seemed like heaven on
the way up, all those I've
loved and lost. And in that
pocket of fog that seemed like
hell when I was in it, the truth
in all things I sighted on the way
that kept me going. I could lean
on this bridge forever but for the
view the next step will bring.

The Inside of Jade

As ancient Buddhists drank tea
to prevent drowsiness during epic
mediations, we drink of each other's
pain and joy to prevent our souls
from going back to sleep.

In the second chapter of Lu Yu's
Cha Ching, the holy scripture of tea,
he remarks that the most potent leaves
have creases that have held the sun
which when softened release
an aroma from the Beginning.

This is what a life ushered into
acceptance looks like: crease,
soften, and in time we unfold
with an ease beyond our making.

The tea hut by design is too
small to enter standing, and too
narrow to bring anything with you.

Like the threshold to wisdom
after a lifetime of trouble.

Under It All

Today, the light is misting
the tops of leaves and the wing
of a finch is stopped by the
sudden warmth

while our dog lifts her face
to the sun, staring into nothing,
sniffing everything, and I glimpse
you watching her, the light
misting your face.

Sometimes, when the mind
sputters, the absolute isness
of life grounds us.

The greatest blessing of love
is being awake at the same time.

Kinship

If you don't know,
then ask the moon in the sky.

—Yuanwu

Trying to prove that all things
are connected is like piling up
snow in a silver bowl.

As soon as you bring it inside,
what you've gathered will vanish.

For truth like the ocean is hard
to see once in it.

I can only say that the things that
matter are always there like stars
in the daytime.

Kindness sleeps in our heart
the way flowers are compressed
in their seed.

Everything is waiting for the right
moment to break ground.

I am always here for you.

Gratitudes

In deep ways, putting words to all that can't be seen is a constant act of gratitude. And so, I'm ever grateful to the shimmers of life that pull me in. Being in conversation there keeps me vital.

I am also grateful to my agent Eve Attermann for her kind, persistent support, and to James Munro, Fiona Baird, and the rest of the WME team. And to Brooke Warner for her vision, kindness, and friendship through the years. And to my publicist Eileen Duhne for her service and enthusiasm.

And deep gratitude to my dear friends who for years have waited while I scribbled and listened while I explored. Especially George, Don, Paul, Skip, TC, David, Parker, Kurt, Pam, Patti, Karen, Paula, Ellen, Dave, Jill, Jacquelyn, Linda, Michelle, Rich, Carolyn, Henk, Elesa, Penny, Sally and Joel. And to Jamie Lee Curtis for being steadfast and true. And to Oprah Winfrey for the walking poem she is.

And to Paul Bowler, who told me I had a voice when we were young. And to Robert Mason, my Homer and Virgil, for always asking the next question. And to my wife, Susan. We met decades ago, by looking into the place that poems open.

—MN

Notes

Quotes and epigraphs without attribution are by the author.

Book One: A Thousand Dawns

p. 7, Staying Afloat, Section Epigraph: "Every day a somewhat different interfusion . . ." Gail Warner. Gail was the founder and director of Pine Manor, a beautiful retreat center in Lake Elsinore in the foothills of Southern CA. She is a wise teacher and a friend. This stanza is from her poem, "Will I Pour Gratitude into Emptiness?" Please see her illustrated book of poems, *Weaving Myself Awake.* Berkeley, CA: She Writes Press, 2017.

p. 57, Path Work, Section: four of the poems in this section originally appeared in other books but begged to be a part of this suite of poems here. They are: "Three Paths" from *Where All the Questions Live,* "Doing and Undoing" from *Seven Thousand Ways to Listen,* "Path Finder" from *A Thirst for Simple Light,* and "What Comes from Being Joined" from *The Chords Under Everything.*

p. 63, To Stand and Serve: "They also serve..." John Milton (1608-1674), the last line of his sonnet "On His Blindness" written in 1655, three years after he went blind at the age of forty-four. Milton later dictated his epic poem, "Paradise Lost," to a series of aides, including his daughter. His master work was first published in 1667, consisting of ten books with over ten thousand lines of verse.

p. 79, The Holy Divide, Section Epigraphs: "The world [is] not to be put in order . . ." Henry Miller, from the journal The Sun, April 2018, Issue 508, p. 48. And **"The transcendence of duality . . ."** Rachel Jamison Webster, from "To Bring into Harmony the Tyger and the Lamb" in *Parabola*, Summer 2016, p. 28.

p. 83, Notes While Meditating: "Gaudi's unfinished cathedral . . ." Antoni Gaudi (1852–1926) was a Catalan architect whose unprecedented structures seemed to portray the elements in flow, as if they were frozen into buildings. He rarely drew his plans but created imaginative, three-dimensional models. From 1915, Gaudi devoted himself almost exclusively to the conception and building of his masterwork, the cathedral in Barcelona known as the Sagrada Família, which I mention here. I first saw this marvel on my trip to Spain in 2004. During Gaudi's life, only the crypt, apse and part of the Nativity facade were completed. Work has continued steadily. The contemporary architect Jordi Bonet i Armengol assumed responsibility in 1987. Completion is not expected until at least 2026.

p. 91, Within: "Within the mountain . . ." Tu Fu, translated by Burton Watson, from "Lovely Lady" in *The Selected Poems of Tu Fu*. NY: Columbia University Press, 2002, p. 52.

p. 94, Wait Long Enough: References to Ch'u Yuan and his lines quoted are from the remarkable anthology, *Classical Chinese Poetry*, translated by David Hinton. NY: Farrar, Straus & Giroux. 2008. pp. 58, 62.

p. 107, Invisible Mirrors, Section Epigraph: "Things may be named . . ." Lao Tzu, from Chapter 1, *Laws Divine and Human (Tao teh Ching)*, translated by Xu Yuanchong, China Intercontinental Press, 2019, p. 2.

p. 123, Coating the Moon, Section Epigraph: "We do not work on dreams..." Josephine Evetts-Secker attributes this thought to James Hillman, cited in "Pictures on My Eyelids: A Jungian Approach to Dreaming" in *Sufi, A Journal of Sufism*. London: Khaniquahi Minatullahi Publications, Issue 97, Summer 2019, p. 14.

p. 145, To Land Wildly, Section Epigraph: "Welcome to the brink of everything ..." Parker J. Palmer, from *On the Brink of Everything: Grace, Gravity, and Getting Old*. CA: Berrett-Koehler, 2018.

p. 154, Tikkun Olam: The Hebrew phrase which means "we are here to repair the world."

p. 156, The Ship of Theseus: Theseus was the mythic king who founded Athens, most known for entering the labyrinth to slay the Minotaur. When Theseus returned from Crete, the Athenians preserved his ship as a sacred museum piece, replacing decayed planks and broken oars over time. The question was raised by Heraclitus and then Plato: With so many parts replaced, was the ship of Theseus still the same boat? This ancient thought experiment was later discussed by Plutarch and, more recently, by Thomas Hobbes and John Locke. A similar story asks, if a grandfather's axe has both its head and handle replaced, is it still the same axe?

p. 160, Looking After: "Embrace it…" Confucius, *The Four Chinese Classics*, translated by David Hinton. Berkeley, CA: Counterpoint. 2013. p. 523.

BOOK TWO: THE GODS VISIT

p. 175, Under the Temple, Section Epigraph: "I know there is no straight road …" Federico Garcia Lorca, from *Four Lorca Suites*, translated by Jerome Rothenberg. Chapbook, Sun and Moon Press, 1989.

p. 193, The Ancient Drift, Section Epigraph: "Think of this One Original Source …" Plotinus, from *Enneads*, III.8.10, cited in the introduction to "The Isha Upanishad" in *The Upanishads*, translated by Eknath Easwaran. CA: Nilgiri Press, 1987, p. 206.

p. 209, Inside the Music Box, Section Epigraph: "To live a spiritual life…" Henri Nouwen, from *Reaching Out: Three Movements of the Spiritual Life*. NY: Image Books, Doubleday, 1986.

p. 227, The One Rain, Section Epigraph: "Perhaps there is a language …" Helen Nearing, from *The Sun*. Chapel Hill, NC, Issue 541, January 2021, p. 48.

p. 243, Close to Finding Our Place, Section Epigraph: "The soul is all things together …" from *The Philosophy of Marsilio Facino* by Kristeller. NY: Columbia University Press, 1943, p. 120. The full quote reads: "The soul is all things together…And since it is the center of all things, it has the forces of all. Hence it passes into all things. And since it is the true connection of all things, it goes to the one without leaving the other… therefore it may rightly be called the center of nature, the middle term of all things, the face of all, the bond and juncture of the universe."

p. 259, The Bottom of Heaven, Section Epigraph: "Let's imagine ourselves …" Robert Mason, from the poem "Private Time" in *Post-Modern Projects*, p. 75.

p. 266, In the poem "A History of Clouds:" "The old samurai turned poet said . . ." Mizuta Masahide (1657–1723) was a Japanese samurai who put down his sword to become a poet and study with Matsuo Basho. His famous haiku, referred to here, is:

> My barn having burned
> to the ground, I can see
> the moon more completely.

p. 274, "The Gods Visit . . ." This poem is inspired by a Japanese print from the Tang Dynasty, "The Gods Visit the Western Mountains," as seen in *Laws Divine and Human (Tao teh Ching)* by Lao Tzu, translated by Xu Yuanchong, China Intercontinental Press, 2019, pp. 53, 54, 56, 57.

BOOK THREE: THE TONE IN THE CENTER OF THE BELL

p. 281, Section Epigraph: "The blood of the children . . ." Pablo Neruda, from the poem "I'm Explaining a Few Things," written in 1936 during the Spanish Civil War, in *Selected Poems: Pablo Neruda*, translated and edited by Nathaniel Tarn. NY: Dell Publishing, 1972.

p. 296, epigraph to "Facing the Question" "Debris does not stay in one place . . ." Rumi, from "Friday" in *The Glance: Songs of Soul-Meeting,* translated by Coleman Barks. NY: Viking/Arkana, 1999, p. 15.

p. 310, epigraph to "What Gate Is This?" "Once through this gateway . . ." Wumen, from *No-Gate Gateway: The Original Wu-Men Kuan,* David Hinton's translation of *The Gateless Gate.* Boston, MA: Shambhala Publications, 2018.

p. 319, Section Epigraph: "If you understand . . ." Hsiang Lin, from *The Blue Cliff Record*, translated by Thomas Cleary and J.C. Cleary. Boston, MA: Shambhala Publications, 2005, Case 17.

p. 321, "The Great Waters" first appeared in the journal, *Sufi*, Winter 2022, Issue 102.

p. 361, Section Epigraph: "I hope you will go out . . ." Clarissa Pinkola Estes.

p. 365, "In the Alley:" This poem first appeared in *Sufi: A Journal of Mystical Philosophy and Practice.* London: Khaniqahi Nimatullahi Publications, Issue 100, Winter 2021.

p. 394, epigraph to "Finding It:" "How will you ever find peace . . ." Rabia, from "The Way the Forest Shelters" in *Love Poems from God*, translated by Daniel Ladinsky. NY: Penguin Compass, 2002, p. 14.

p. 399, epigraph to "Kinship:" "If you don't know . . ." The epigraph to this poem is a line from the commentary in the 13th case (koan), "Piling Up Snow in a Silver Bowl," in *The Blue Cliff Record,* the classic text of 100 koans compiled and unfolded by the Chan master Yuanwu Keqin in 1125. The metaphor I explore in the first two stanzas is in tribute to Yuanwu and his deep insight.

About the Author

With over a million copies sold, MARK NEPO has moved and inspired readers and seekers all over the world with his #1 *New York Times* bestseller *The Book of Awakening*. Beloved as a poet, teacher, and storyteller, Mark has been called "one of the finest spiritual guides of our time," "a consummate storyteller," and "an eloquent spiritual teacher." His work is widely accessible and used by many and his books have been translated into more than twenty languages.

A bestselling author, he has published twenty-four books and recorded sixteen audio projects. In 2015, he was given a Life-Achievement Award by AgeNation. In 2016, he was named by *Watkins: Mind Body Spirit* as one of the 100 Most Spiritually Influential Living People, and was also chosen as one of OWN's *Super-Soul 100*, a group of inspired leaders using their gifts and voices to elevate humanity. And In 2017 Mark became a regular columnist for *Spirituality & Health Magazine*.

Recent work includes *Falling Down and Getting Up* (St. Martin's Essentials, 2023); *Surviving Storms* (St. Martin's Essentials, 2022); *The Book of Soul* (St. Martin's Essentials, 2020), a Nautilus Book Award Winner; *Drinking from the River of Light* (Sounds True, 2019), a Nautilus Book Award Winner; *More Together Than Alone* (Atria, 2018) cited by *Spirituality & Practice* as one of the Best Spiritual Books of 2018; *Things That*

Join the Sea and the Sky (Sounds True, 2017), a Nautilus Book Award Winner; *The Way Under the Way: The Place of True Meeting* (Sounds True, 2016), a Nautilus Book Award Winner; *The One Life We're Given* (Atria) cited by Spirituality & Practice as one of the Best Spiritual Books of 2016, *Inside the Miracle* (Sounds True) selected by *Spirituality & Health Magazine* as one of the top ten best books of 2015; *The Endless Practice* (Atria) cited by *Spirituality & Practice* as one of the Best Spiritual Books of 2014; and *Seven Thousand Ways to Listen* (Atria), which won the 2012 Books for a Better Life Award.

Mark was part of Oprah Winfrey's *The Life You Want Tour* in 2014 and has appeared several times with Oprah on her *Super Soul Sunday* program on OWN TV. He has also been interviewed by Robin Roberts on *Good Morning America*. *The Exquisite Risk* was listed by *Spirituality & Practice* as one of the Best Spiritual Books of 2005, calling it "one of the best books we've ever read on what it takes to live an authentic life."

Mark devotes his writing and teaching to the journey of inner transformation and the life of relationship. He continues to offer readings, lectures, and retreats. Please visit Mark at: MarkNepo.com, threeintentions.com, and harrywalker.com/speakers/mark-nepo.

Permissions

Thorough efforts have been made to secure all permissions. Any omissions or corrections will be made in future editions.

Thanks for permission to reprint excerpts from the following previously published works:

BOOK ONE:

A Thousand Dawns

Excerpt from Gail Warner's poem "Will I Pour Gratitude into Emptiness?" from her book, *Weaving Myself Awake*. By permission of She Writes Press.

Excerpt from *Selected Poems of Du Fu*, translated by Burton Watson. Copyright 2003. Reprinted with permission of Columbia University Press.

Excerpt from Parker J. Palmer's book, *On the Brink of Everything: Grace, Gravity, and Getting Old*. By permission of Berrett-Koehler Publishers.

Excerpt from Confucius, *The Four Classics*, translated by David Hinton. By permission of Counterpoint Press.

BOOK TWO:

The Gods Visit

Excerpt from Federico Garcia Lorca, from *Four Lorca Suites*, translated by Jerome Rothenberg. Chapbook, 1989.

BOOK THREE:

The Tone in the Center of The Bell

Excerpt from Pablo Neruda, from the poem "I'm Explaining a Few Things," in *Selected Poems: Pablo Neruda*, translated and edited by Nathaniel Tarn. NY: Dell Publishing, 1972.

"In the Alley" and "In Those Moments" first appeared in *Sufi: A Journal of Mystical Philosophy and Practice*. London: Khaniqahi Nimatullahi Publications, Issue 100, Winter 2021.

Excerpt from Rumi, from the poem "Friday" in *The Glance: Songs of Soul-Meeting,* translated by Coleman Barks. Permission of Viking/Arkana Publishing.

Excerpt from "Gatha" by Wu-Men Kuan, from No-Gate Gateway translated by David Hinton. Translation copyright © 2018 by David Hinton. Reprinted with the permission of The Permissions Company, LLC on behalf of Shambhala Publications Inc., Boulder, CO. shambhala.com.

About Freefall Books

Throughout my life, I have been blessed to be prolific. In large part, this is because I am compelled to write about what I don't know. If I only wrote about what I know, I would have written very little. I have also been blessed to have wonderful publishers and editors over the years with whom I still work and publish.

With Freefall Books, I can share books that have not been able to find a home in the commercial publishing world. This imprint allows me the creative freedom to bring to you compelling roads of inquiry in books that have served as teachers for me.

I would describe the theme of Freefall Books this way: Before you can fly, you have to welcome falling. It is the in between space that calls us to open our heart and spread our wings. It is the in between space that is transformative and life-giving. For there is always a moment between falling and flying where we are most deeply instructed about life.

Freefall Books is devoted to the exploration of that deeply instructive moment—however it appears—and to the covenant of care, best expressed by the Renaissance philosopher Pico Mirandola. In 1486, after writing 900 theses to explore the unity of religion, philosophy, nature, and magic, Pico concluded that "friendship is the end of all philosophy."

I am grateful to my dear friend, Brooke Warner, a writer and publisher in her own right, for her help, guidance, and company in creating this imprint. And to my oldest friend, Robert Mason, for his endless support and birdlike ability to see. And to my most intimate friend, my wife, Susan McHenry, who watered the seed of this dream many years ago.

—MN

Freefall

If you have one hour of air
and many hours to go,
you must breathe slowly.

If you have one arm's length
and many things to care for,
you must give freely.

If you have one chance to know God
and many doubts, you must
set your heart on fire.

We are blessed.

Each day is a chance.
We have two arms.
Fear wastes air.

—MN